Poetry and Prophecy

To those who speak to the many deaf ears attend.
To those who speak to one,
In poet's song and song of bird,
Many listen; but the voice that speaks to none
By all is heard:
Sound of the wind, music of the stars, prophetic word.

Kathleen Raine

TABLE OF CONTENTS

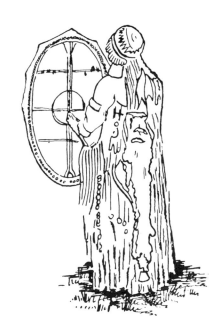

Lindisfarne Letter

Copyright © 1979 by the Lindisfarne Assoc
All rights reserved
The Lindisfarne Letter is published by the
Lindisfarne Press, RD2, West Stockbridge
Mass. for members of the Association.

HARVEST OF LEARNING I HAVE REAPED

Harvest of learning I have reaped,
Fruits of many a life-time stored,
The false discarded, proven kept,
Knowledge that is its own reward—
    No written page more true
    Than blade of grass and drop of dew.

Striven my partial self to bind
Within tradition great and whole,
Christendom's two thousand years,
Wisdom's universal mind—
    No doctrine heart can heal
    As cloudless sky and lonely hill.

Now I am old my books I close
And forget religion's ties,
Untrammelled the departing soul
Puts out of mind both false and true,
    Distant hills and spacious skies,
    Grass-blade and morning dew.
                Kathleen Raine

Kathleen Raine: An Introduction

CHRISTOPHER BAMFORD

This issue of the Lindisfarne Letter is offered to Dr. Kathleen Raine, who was Scholar-in-Residence during our last semester in Manhattan.

Dr. Raine is British: a poet, scholar, critic and philosopher. Now in her seventies, she is the author of eight books of poetry, an autobiography in three volumes, and several works of scholarly and philosophical criticism whose central concern has been the re-affirmation of what she believes to be the perennial, true and spiritual ground of poetry and inspiration. In this guise, Dr. Raine delivered her seminal Mellon Lectures on Blake and Tradition and, more recently, while at Lindisfarne, gave her "Summa Blakeana"—her lectures on Blake's *Illustrations of the Book of Job*. In such projects, as indeed in all her work, Dr. Raine has constantly striven to elucidate the sacramental wisdom of the imagination, that wisdom inherent in reality, immanent in nature and in mind, which the poet, when he or she is most truly "original", only uncovers or remembers. This symbolic gnosis, "of form and beauty inviolate", in which "inner and outer reality are at one, the world in harmony with the imagination", is, Dr. Raine believes, humanity's original and natural state—the Earthly Paradise or Eden, which each must recover or else perish, but which once restored becomes its own joy, true science and true poetry:

> Sleep at the tree's root, where the
> night is spun
> Into the stuff of worlds, listen to
> the winds,

> The tides, and the night's harmonies,
> and know
> All that you knew before you
> began to forget...
> (*Message from Home*)

Convinced of the primacy of the imagination—that mental things alone are real—Dr. Raine's life and work have been concerned with tracing, learning and practicing this one journey of remembrance, the narrow track the soul must tread, from Eden to Eden, through all the hells, until end and beginning joined once more, hells transcended and illusion dropped away, the perfection of the original sphere—"the cell and seed of life"—is wrought again. "Poetry," Dr. Raine states repeatedly, "is the language of the soul," invoking by this distinction the traditional tripartite anthropology of body, soul and spirit (or intellect). For it is the soul, in Christianity and in Platonism, whose descent becomes a fall through self-love when, as an image enamoured of itself, it becomes entangled in the suffering that follows from thinking that it is substantial in itself, its own source. And so it is the soul and its world, fallen and de-symbolised, which must be purified and educated so that, raised up and reunited with its celestial double, its true original, it can raise the world up and transform its veil of illusion into the diaphonous and redemptive play of symbols:

> Bright cloud,
> Bringer of rain to far fields,
> To me, who will not drink that water-
> fall nor feel
> Wet mist on my face,
> White gold and rose
> Vision of light,

> *Meaning and beauty immeasurable.*
> *That meaning is not rain, nor that*
>   *beauty mist.*
>   (*Bright Cloud*)

The drama of the soul then, whose language is poetry, is that of life itself, of created things and of our earthly being, of the struggle to recall and, recalling, to unite with that higher principle which Dr. Raine, following Plato and Yeats, calls the Daimon. Indeed, Dr. Raine feels with Plato that poetry and life, if they do not recall and lead us back to Eden—if they do not partake of the "inner journey"—are abused and have no true place in the ideal Republic. For Dr. Raine, as for all Platonists, life and art—social, ethical and aesthetic (as also biological and physical) forms—have but one function, the perfection of being which is the knowledge and remembrance of the Eternal Kingdom:

> *Their only task to recollect*
> *Originals laid up in heaven...*
>   (*Ninfa Revisited*)

Dr. Raine's first guide in this was her life itself, inscribed like a palimpsest with the century's great themes of loss and anguish, rootlessness and passion, reductionism and materialism—all these borne witness to, overcome and transformed by a continuous striving to be in all things true to herself, her vision and sacred calling. Next, Blake and Yeats (and to a lesser degree Keats, Shelley, Coleridge, Dante, Spenser and Milton) led her to drink deeply at the "ancient springs" of Platonism, Hermeticism and Kabbalah, teaching her to attend closely to such perennial "singing masters of the soul" as Orpheus, Plato, Hermes, Plotinus, Porphyry, Iamblichus, Proclus, Paracelsus, Boehme, Swedenborg and Thomas Taylor. Long labor in this school confirmed that Blake and Yeats were not at all "original" in the modern sense, but were fully so in the ancient one; were not innovators, except in the precise etymological sense of those who "renewed",

that is made new again for their time what was perennially and continuously new: the wisdom and process of creation itself. Realizing this, Dr. Raine has worked to recover the possibility of such a "renewal" or gnosis—that remembering which Plato called a "not-forgetting"—both for herself and for her age. It was always this that spurred her on; and her study and her scholarship were always secondary to it— "always incidental to the needs of a poet for knowledge of a certain kind." Thus she never fitted easily into an academic role and mostly worked on her own, outside and for herself. "Like Thomas Taylor," she writes, "I read the books of wisdom for the sake of that wisdom, seeing scholarship always as a means to an end, never as an end in itself":

> *Stone into man must grow, the human word*
> *carved by our whispers in the passing air*
>
> *is the authentic utterance of cloud,*
> *the speech of flowing water, blowing wind,*
> *of silver moon and stunted juniper.*
>   (*Night in Martindale*)

Indeed, Dr. Raine is perhaps most precious to us because she is so much what she teaches—which means that one cannot agree with her philosophy and remain untouched by her life, or admire her scholarship but deplore her philosophy. Her poetry, her life, her metaphysics, her aesthetics, her cosmology are all of one piece, a single seamless cloth. It is this wholeness that has allowed her to be one of those to perform for our time the same function that Pythagoras, Plato, Plotinus, Proclus, Eriugena, Ficino and Thomas Taylor performed for their's—the living transmission of the Orphic Teaching. By this count the eighth in the succession, Dr. Raine may be said to mark the beginning of a new octave; and this, though fanciful, is at least metaphorically apt. For by virtue of never forgetting the inner need of her soul to find a teaching appropriate to it, and by stubbornly refusing the step of crossing religious boundaries to accept the wisdom and method of another tradition, while at the same time—though converting to Roman Catholicism—finding herself deeply incapable of accepting Christianity in its historical aspect, Dr. Raine has become a prophet of that "new age" of the spirit in which the only true authority is the wisdom of the heart, Blake's True Man, the Imagination. Led to this view by her life as by her study, Dr. Raine was also brought to confront its logical complement, the simultaneous reality of an ending, of what she calls "the leaf-fall of a civilization"— the natural term of European Christendom. From this stance on the cusp, she faces the end of the twentieth century with both hope for a new civilization and the fear of a terrible barbarism—the hope lying with "the seeds, the living among the dead, those who do not participate in the collective disintegration, but guard their secret of immortality, the essence of what has been and may be again", and the barbarism, the chaotic disintegration within which these seeds will germinate, lying among those who have no knowledge of "what has been and may be again", and so have no past or ground, either ontological or historical:

> *To be a barbarian is to have no past;*
> *For the past is the present of the*
> *future, the human kingdom;*
> *Some known to us, others unknown,*
> *you, I, that still continuing few*
> *To whose hearts the remembered and*
> *forgotten dead are presences,*
> *Ripening in memory the seed of cities*
> *To scatter for what meagre crop this*
> *poisoned stricken earth may bear,*
> *Or harvest into that native land*
> *we desire and remember,*
> *Keep France, keep Christendom,*
> *keep Athens in mind.*
> *(Letter to Pierre Emmanuel)*

Here Dr. Raine deeds us another gift— her understanding of culture as that net of truths that a society must hold permanent so that others may be changed, as the society itself changes, endures change, and yet remains the same. These are the qualities that ensure continuity and order, the invisible bonds of shared value, humanly honed and perfected and passed on in innumerable ways, whose embodiment is both a practice and a gnosis, a living access to the knowledge sub specie aeternitatis that myth, ritual, history and literature transmit and evoke. Without such a cultural tradition, as the Russian poet Mandelstam realized when he underwent what Dr. Raine calls "the Marxist variant of our Western materialism", history (and evolution) becomes "mere progress"—"the mechanical movement of a clock-hand, not the sacred succession of interlinked events".

Finally, and perhaps most precious of all, there is the poetry in which for half a century Dr. Raine has kept true to herself in language true to itself, writing a poetry not dictated by the fashions of the moment but inwardly determined by what she experienced as the unifying links that bind the human soul to the larger cosmos whose she is and must strive to reveal. This, in a sense, is sacred poetry, the paradox and promise of which is prophetically revealed in her first collected poem—which, as it should, resumes and stands as an introduction to the rest:

> *A bird sings on a matin tree*
> *'Once such a bird was I.'*
>
> *The sky's gaze says*
> *'Remember your mother.'*
>
> *Seas, trees and voices cry*
> *'Nature is your nature.'*
>
> *I reply*
> *'I am what is not what I was.*
> *Seas, trees, and bird, alas!*
> *Sea, tree, and bird was I.'*
> *(Lyric)*

Prophecy and Poetry

WILLIAM IRWIN THOMPSON
KATHLEEN RAINE

*Remarks on the Esoteric Tradition
in a Symposium on W.B. Yeats,
at Lindisfarne in Manhattan
9 November 1978*

William Irwin Thompson

I thought that it would be appropriate, in this last semester of our program of "Lindisfarne in Manhattan," to honor Kathleen Raine (who has been living with us for the last two months as our Scholar-in-Residence) by having this symposium on W. B. Yeats. By having this evening of homage to the old great spirit of Yeats, we are acknowledging that Yeats is the source of motivation for much of all our work; certainly, in the case of Lindisfarne, Yeats is a teacher in the school we all attend.

I think that if one stops to consider Yeats as a spiritual guide as well as a great poet, then one has to recognize that great artists and geniuses place a burden upon us not simply to study them, or do research on them, but to live them, to continue their work, to express a passionate, embodied knowledge. Yeats, like all great men, can become the foundation for an enormous scholarly industry, of a thousand doctoral dissertations (and I am certainly guilty of one of those dissertations on Yeats and the 1916 Rising), but to balance all that scholarly concern for the letter with a cultural concern for the spirit, we must do more than perform research on Yeats, we must take him seriously by embodying his knowledge in life. The first step in taking Yeats seriously is to take the Esoteric Tradition seriously. The political critics of Yeats, like George Orwell, tried to dismiss Yeats's "tomfoolery of wheels and gyres," but the difficulty with the political critics of Yeats, be they George Orwell or Conor Cruise O'Brien, is that they are too limited by the provincial viewpoint of materialism, scientific or dialectical. Yeats cannot be understood within the limitations of that narrow tradition, for the Esoteric Tradition upon which he draws is more universal. Like Blake before him, Yeats understood that the Esoteric is what lies above and beyond culture; in fact, from the spiritual level of consciousness, culture itself is simply the strategy of one specific historical time and place to incarnate the divine and cosmic consciousness. So, it was no accident that Yeats began his career by publishing an edition of the works of William Blake. In working to revive Blake, Yeats was working to bring to the surface of the global British Empire the underground streams of the Esoteric Tradition that have nourished every great civilization, from ancient Egypt to industrial England.

Poets like Blake or Yeats realized that every civilization is based upon a vision: whether the vision comes from Buddha sitting under the Boddhi Tree, from Mohammed in his cave, or from Jesus on the mount with Moses and Elijah, the vision is an attempt to body forth in the politics of time, the politics of eternity. When one receives or inherits a vision, one cannot simply study it, or do research on it; one has to embody it. The Word must become flesh, first in the individual body, then in the body-politic. That embodiment requires not simply the mechanical repetition of the vision, but the re-creation in every generation of the Esoteric Tradition in a wholly novel way. One simply cannot clone the Esoteric; it is unique, for the way in which it embodies the universal is in the individual life. One cannot manufacture the Esoteric in universities or churches, one has to reincarnate it in a wholly novel historical context. The proper response to Blake is W. B. Yeats. The proper response to Yeats is Kathleen Raine.

In my own and more limited way the burden that I picked up from Yeats required shifting the weight of emphasis from academic research *on* Yeats to cultural work in the spirit *of* Yeats. In being a university teacher and taking the Old Man seriously, I had to ask myself: "Isn't there some way in which the Humanities can be lived in a new way: not in the way of the classroom where *A Vision* is either patronized or dismissed, but in the meditation room where the truths behind *A Vision* are experienced first hand?" When one has a personal experience of the Esoteric, then one can see that the eternal modes are mythic and archetypal and stand outside of time, but that they do touch history as history becomes the performance of myth. The music comes out of silence but is performed in time.

In each generation the Esoteric Tradition has not died, but has been recreated. Think of it in terms of Weber's sociology: the exoteric is the routinization of charisma. In this cultural process the artist becomes the foundation of a scholarly industry, the saint becomes the foundation of a religious order or a sect. The exoteric has its place, for the copies of the poems of Yeats or the Gospels of Jesus that we have in our libraries come from an exoteric process of publication. But the Esoteric Tradition is a direct teaching that comes from beyond time; it is the teaching that comes from the disincarnate guru, the figure known as "the Green Man" in Islam, or Melchizedek in Christianity. Some of Yeats's works come from exoteric sources of inspiration, from reading the works of Swedenborg, Blake, or William Morris; but some of the sources of inspiration for Yeats come from direct and personal encounter with the Esoteric.

Now, the usual way in which we treat our great figures, saints, artists, or statesmen, is to canonize them, and by canonizing them render them impotent so that we can ignore them through lip service and ritual. The best way to ignore Ghandi, after Nehru's fashion in the industrialization of India, is to make Ghandi a saint, put his picture on the wall of every school, and then feel free to turn away from his thought in cottage industries and economic decentralization to develop capital-intensive economies of scale and the industrial momentum that will eventually lead to India's development of the atom bomb. And now, in much the same exoteric way, China is about to do to Mao what India did to Ghandi, or we did to Jefferson. China is importing *Coca-Cola*, MacDonalds, and Wonder-Bread, and moving in with them are high-rise apartments, traffic jams, and smog. In the exoteric process of cultural dissemination one has the routinization of charisma, the experience of the *enantiodromia* in which things turn into their opposites; in the Esoteric Tradition of the reincarnation of the Word, one has the reversal of the reversal, the charismatic transformation of institutional routines.

Because there are contradictions built into the dynamics of our institutions, our institutions continually need to die and be reborn. I think that, perhaps, one good vision of this is to consider where we are now. This is a historical landmark church of New York; it has a long history behind it, long, at least, for America. It is where the complete organ works of Bach were first performed in the United States; it is also where the Easter Parade originated. This used to be the fashionable district, where the department stores were, and so the custom developed of walking after church in a parade of celebration, a celebration of wealth and position. This was an extremely fashionable church in the nineteenth century, but now, of course, it is coming apart and the plaster is falling off the walls. There are too many historical landmarks in New York for citizens and philanthropists to restore them all, so bit by bit the energy needed for a city to recreate itself must go to all the immediate crises that absorb its attention. So the landmarks sit, like old car wrecks on the expressways, as metaphors of a civilization gone to entropy.

As a historical vision of one relationship between the sacred and the secular, between the Protestant Ethic and the spirit of capitalism, the landmark we are sitting in is an expression of an old form of life, but if the Parish had not died it would never have become open for new forms of life, like Lindisfarne, to come in. So there are times when the rib cage of a dead animal can become the trellis for flowers. When we try to resist death, we lock energies into a weak form, and we might say, thermodynamically, make them unavailable for work. The best way to make life available for work is to allow it to move to its own proper death, to let the supernova scatter the atomic material of a dying star to seed newly evolving solar systems. It is much the same with our institutions. We have to know how to come to terms with the death of an institution, a church or a university, or even something larger, a city or a civilization.

As far as I am able to see, we really are experiencing the supernova of New York. New York is a tremendous vision of one kind of civilization, of a civilization built upon the hierarchy of money and power; the World Trade Center or the Citicorp Bank, with the little church of St. Peter's neatly tucked under its arm, says it all. New York is the solar plexus of our industrial civilizational system; it is a chakra in the subtle body of this world-epoch. But as many mystics, prophets, and artists have already told us, that civilizational system is changing, and the very subtle body of the earth is going through an initiation in which the old is coming apart and the new is being formed. As that happens, everything changes, the collective unconscious of the race, as well as the weather. Those who are insensitive to these changes, or those who feel them in their souls but resist them in their egos, insist that New York is still powerful and great and will continue for all the time they care about. It is their world, after all, and so, small wonder that they cannot stand to see it change. But when you hold something in your hand too tightly, you kill it. Thus those who are rigid and resist change, ironically, create the rigidity that causes the system to break apart.

Yeats was right, the center cannot hold. None of the centers of civilization can, for they have become the centers of contradiction. We live now in the phase of "Hunchback, Saint, and Fool," and have only twenty-five years or so before the whole *Magnus Annus* has played itself out. Yeats made his prophecies over fifty years ago, but most people were taught to read Yeats's visionary system as a device that helped Yeats develop some original metaphors; had the critics been better educated they would have known that Yeats's visionary system was not original at all; it was the heritage of a long-established prophetic lineage. Within that prophetic tradition, Yeats is more relevant today than he was in his own day. If anyone speaks to us in the conditions of the latter days of the declining twentieth century, it is certainly Yeats. He is at once the figure who sums up everything about the culture that is passing and points to a wholly new culture that is coming. He was not a fascist, but a true *radical* whose roots went down into the underground streams of our Western Civilization: down into Blake and Swedenborg, down further into Boehme, into Ficino, down further into medieval alchemy, and further back into Alexandrian Hermeticism, and through them into the bedrock of Pythagoras and Orpheus. If we truly appreciate the breadth and depth of Yeats's vision, and if we accept his bardic, prophetic gifts, but do not turn him into a plaster of Paris saint, then I think that we will begin to realize that his knowledge is a tough knowledge to survive. Very little of one's easy and confident faith in contemporary civilization can survive the elemental touch of Yeats's terrible beauty.

I would like to close my remarks about Yeats as a prophet by reading two quotations from the *Letters* of Yeats, for I think that these two statements truly address themselves to the crisis of the modern world-system. The first is from a letter to Ethel Mannin on April 8, 1936:

> *Do not try to make a politician of me. Even in Ireland, I shall never, I think, be that again. As my sense of reality deepens, and I think it does with age, my horror at the cruelty of governments grows greater. And if I did what you want, I would seem to hold one form of government more responsible than any other, and that would betray my convictions. Communist, fascist, nationalist, clerical, anti-clerical are all responsible according to the number of their victims. I have not been silent; I have used the only vehicle I possess, verse. If you have my poems by you, look upon a poem called, "The Second Coming." It was written some sixteen or seventeen years ago, and foretold what is happening. I have written of the same thing*

again and again since. This will seem little to you with your strong practical sense, for it takes fifty years for a poet's weapons to influence the issue.

Well, I think in 1986 we will remember W. B. Yeats.

This is from one of the last letters Yeats wrote, just a few weeks before his death. In it, I think, he expresses a vision of the harmony of opposites that, if we make it through this apocalyptic transition from one world-system to another, then in should become the basis for a new vision of polity, of a new world polity. This was written to Lady Elizabeth Pelham on January 4, 1939:

> *I know for certain that my time will not be long. I have put away everything that can be put away that I may speak what I have to speak. And I find expression is a part of study. In two or three weeks, I am now idle that I may rest after writing much verse, I will begin to write my most fundamental thoughts, and the arrangement of thought which I am convinced will complete my studies. I am happy and I think full of an energy, of an energy I had despaired of. It seems to me that I have found what I wanted. When I try to put it all into a phrase, I say: "Man can embody Truth, but he cannot know it." I must embody it in the completion of my life. The abstract is not life and everywhere draws out its contradictions. You can refute Hegel, but not the saint or the Song of Sixpence.*

By taking Yeats seriously we can realize that one cannot know the truth, for that presumption is the arrogance of the ego, the ego that tries to possess the infinite by saying, "This is mine." *My* possession, *my* opinion. But one can experience the Truth by embodying one perspective of it. The way in which the Truth of the whole expresses itself is in the dance of opposites.

Truth cannot be expressed in a single ideology; it cannot be expressed in capitalism or communism, or any other popular *ism*. The truth expresses itself in the dance of opposites, and if one accepts the wisdom of Blake, that "In opposition is true friendship," then one can see that even an opponent can become a necessary complement. The opponent or enemy draws one forth into the achievement of one's own excellence, one's *arete*. In combatting the opponent one achieves what is most noble in one position, and in that moment of nobility, recognizes the nobility in the opponent's position. This recognition is but another version of Jesus's admonition to love one's enemy. A politics that would be based upon this dance of opposites could not be a single, monolithic world-state, a single monolithic world-economy, a single monolithic world-religion, or a single monolithic world ideology. Such an enantiomorphic world polity would have to be more like an ecosystem, a complex interaction of different entities and agents in a dance in which each required all. Capitalist would counter but affirm communist as the beach counters but affirms the sea, or as the mountains counter but affirm the clouds. I believe the creation of such an enantiomorphic world polity is the only hope for the survival of the human race.

H. G. Wells said that the future was a race between catastrophe and education. Now as catastrophe seems to be outracing education, we need to realize that there is perhaps a shorter distance to our goal, that if we exhaust ourselves by chasing in the same direction as catastrophe we will never catch up. Now that the universities have joined the arms-race, we need a new kind of education that runs in a different direction, perhaps a kind of education that does not run at all, but sits *zazen*. What Yeats or the Buddhists are calling upon us to understand is the limit to the ego, and

since civlization is the ego of human culture, the limit to civilization. If we are going to experience the death of the ego, then we are also collectively going to experience the death of civilization. But out of that death and transformation will come a new incarnation, a new polity unimaginable in terms of our industrial civilization: a harmony of nature and culture, ecology and consciousness beyond anything that New York can possibly express, for New York is the consumate expression of the vanishing civilization. Yeats's letter before his own death is an instruction to us on how to die; but, of course, we need to realize that only Life can teach us that: death cannot teach us how to die.

Kathleen Raine

I came to Lindisfarne two months ago, feeling that it was perhaps one of the very few places on this planet where one can speak of these things openly and without pretense. I think most of you come to Lindisfarne for the same reason. We are looking for values other than those given us by the contemporary world, as Bill Thompson has so eloquently said. Those values seem to me to be embodied in the thought of Yeats more completely than in any other poet. I remember very well when I was young (I was in my twenties) that Yeats was already thought to be a very old-fashioned poet because he wrote in strict verse form rather than in the new free verse of Eliot, of Ezra Pound, of the symbolists. Later Yeats was attacked by Auden and the school of the political poets of the twenties because, as they said, he showed no concern for the leading ideas of his generation: as if the leading ideas of the greatest poet of his generation were, at any time, not the leading ideas! Whose ideas if not Yeats's were the ideas that are seminal and that we should follow?

Now we have seen the bankruptcy of many things, and begin to understand what it is that Yeats is asking of us. He, of course, was not original; no great writer is ever original. Every great revival, every great progress in the arts is, in a literal sense, a renaissance, a rebirth; and that which is reborn is always and everywhere the same universal knowledge and wisdom. We have grown up to think that there are certain laws in the realm of material science which any age, studying chemistry, studying physiology, studying astronomy, would rediscover. For some reason we have not realized that spiritual laws are no less strict, no less universal, no less inevitably discovered and rediscovered.

One has been hearing for some time the phrase, "the New Age", the "Age of Aquarius", but what is this New Age? Some people think that it means going into outer space on rockets, populating the moon, putting platforms to float around the earth where people will live in some sort of computer. Yeats understood that a New Age is not just more and more of what we already have, of more and more discovery in the order of the material sciences, impressive as that may be. We live at the end of a great age of scientific discovery, which itself began at the end of a great age of scholasticism, of the intellectual edifices of theology and the Church. Yeats understood that the New Age is not what is thought of by evolutionists as progress. Popular scientism seems persuaded that evolution is the product of the chance bombardment of mindless molecules, but that nonetheless this chance process is bound to produce Utopia. Why, one wonders, if all is the work of blind chance, should the evolutionist, paradoxically, have so much faith in this Utopia which evolution is "inevitably" going to produce?

Yeats was not original in writing about a New Age; as a young man he had himself trained his mind on Blake. Ellis and Yeats's edition, in 1893, was the first edition of Blake's Prophetic Books, which had lain unpublished since his death sixty-five years earlier. Blake had proclaimed a New Age, which was to see a rebirth of spirit, and was to be the last age of the world, the coming of the kingdom of the Imagination, which Blake called the Divine Humanity. Blake himself was following Swedenborg, the eighteenth century visionary, who had himself proclaimed the coming of age of humanity in the Church of the New Jerusalem. Bill Thompson would call it the Church of the Fourth Gospel, the Mystical Gospel of Saint John. Whereas the evolutionists see their Utopia as an extension and continuation of current world trends, a society in which material science will have found solutions to all problems and fulfilled all human needs (the needs of natural man, that is), Blake, Yeats and Swedenborg proclaimed a reversal of the premises of our civilization. This is very difficult for us to envisage, so conditioned is all our thought by current ideas of progress in material fields, of unlimited scientific discovery. Yeats, however, returned to the pre-Socratic and Platonic view of the Great Year, whose phases of civilization are dominated in turn by the eternal opposites, matter and spirit, Iron Age and Golden Age. "Things thought too long can be no longer thought", and there is a principle of enantiodromia, which decrees that when we have gone so far in one direction, the pendulum must swing back in the opposite direction. The "months" of the Great Year are, according to astrological calculations, of some two thousand years' duration; and according to Yeats's diagram, set out in his work *A Vision*, we have (as Bill Thompson has said) perhaps only twenty-five or fifty years more of the kind of world we know. We are ripe for a change of premises; and already the birth of the New Age, symbolically represented by the precession of the equinox from Pisces to Aquarius, is beginning to take place, here and there, and with increasing insistence. Lindisfarne bears its witness to this change, is a part of this manifestation.

Plato, you remember, spoke of two ages, the Golden and the Iron Ages of the world. In the Golden Age, God conducts the world, and the spiritual humanity prevails, the "Golden Race"; then after myriads of revolutions, God lets go the reins of government and the world unwinds like a tightly wound spring when it is released, running down of its own accord, not conducted by God; and this is the Iron Age, in which the earth-born men prevail, the natural man not the spiritual man, called by Blake and Swedenborg the Divine Humanity. With a reversal of the gyres comes a reversal of values; and Yeats wrote of the "rise of soul against intellect" now beginning in the world. In the New Age the assumption of materialism, that matter is the ground and basis of reality, that the only causes are material causes, will be challenged; the power and the reality of spiritual causes will be once more discovered. A rediscovery of spiritual things will mark the character of the New Age, as Blake and Yeats understood it.

Yeats, much mocked by the clever young men of my own generation, studied, scanned the whole horizon, one may say, of the new knowledge which was to form the ground of the new age which he saw coming into existence. That knowledge is, from the point of view of our present civilization, an excluded knowledge: nobody speaks of it in the Universities; there is a tacit censorship of many areas of experience which are not, according to the materialist premises, knowledge at all. I was myself much surprised when in some academic circles my own studies in the fields of excluded knowledge (excluded, that is, in official academic circles, but in truth the ground of the thought and the works of Blake and Yeats, Shelley and Coleridge, to say nothing of Goethe and indeed of the Romantic movement as a whole) were received with bitter hostility; received values and those who sustain those values were under threat; and whereas I had imagined that many would in the reaffirmation of spiritual values see not a threat but a release, I was surprised to discover how few shared my sense of being shown a greater world. That is one reason that has brought me to Lindisfarne, where it is possible to speak without censorship of themes which are the perennial concern of poets but not, as I discovered, of their academic commentators; of whom there are many who would like to see Blake's and Yeats's spiritual knowledge swept back as quickly as possible under the carpet; not to have these fields of thought spoken of or written of, but on the contrary to falsify the works of the poets in order to make them seem to conform with the received ideas of a secular materialist society.

Yeats came to this knowledge first not

through Blake but through Blake's own teacher, Swedenborg; a name seldom mentioned in academic circles, but called by the great French philosopher and orientalist Henri Corbin, in whose recent death we sustain so great a loss, the Buddha of Western Europe. That may be an exaggeration; but he was the first teacher of Blake and of Yeats, their contact with universal tradition and the first prophet of the change of premises in our world which we now begin to see. Blake knew only the Western esoteric tradition—Alchemy, Christian Cabbala, and, above all, Neoplatonism through the translations made by his contemporary and at one time friend Thomas Taylor, the Platonist, whose influence upon the American Transcendentalists was no less great and continuing. By the time of Yeats, other tributaries were flowing into this mainstream. Through H. P. Blavatsky's writings and influence, Egyptian studies and the first influx of Indian metaphysics and theology began to be felt. Yeats's intention was most serious in studying all those fields of knowledge which, like both the Indian religions (Buddhism and Vedanta), take mind and not matter to be the ground and first principle. Early studies in magic and his lifelong investigations in the field of psychical research (studies characterised by a critical objectivity remote from the credulity once attributed to him by his uncomprehending critics) were motivated by this purpose of discovering the nature and the laws of mind. In later life he made deep studies of Plato, and of Plotinus's writings in the beautiful translation of his fellow-Irishman Stephen Mackenna. In the Indian dance, in the No theatre of Japan, he found art-forms rooted in a philosophy of mind. At the end of his life Yeats reached what we may call his final destination in the grand and all-embracing teachings of Vedanta. With his Indian teacher, Shri Purohit Swami, he translated the six principal Upanishads and the Bhagavad Geeta. In all these varied studies, from Irish folk-beliefs to the philosophy of Plotinus and Shankara, we can now see that Yeats prepared for us a map of the interior regions which seem likely to concern the New Age; for all are related by a common theme—the reality of mind, or spirit, as the ground and first princple of the universe. In many respects it is the programme of Lindisfarne that he mapped out; with the one exception of ecology, without which, however, it is possible that there might be a total destruction of the civilized world, and therefore no possibility of carrying out the spiritual development Yeats foresaw as the theme of the Age of Aquarius.

It seems very clear now that Yeats was right when he declared that the "three provincial centuries", from Descartes to whomever you like to name among the great culture-heroes of science, are over, and that the rise of soul against intellect (or rationalist thought based upon the premises of a materialist science) is indeed now beginning in the world. He called those centuries provincial, of course, in the light of the unanimous and universal tradition of the *Sophia Perennis* to be restored in the New Age.

The alternation of the gyres is one symbol which may describe what we see coming about; another, which we cannot forget, is that we are witnessing the last phase of what the Vedanta calls the Kali-Yuga, and the Hebrew tradition the end of days. Either way the responsibility lies with us to use the time given us in the restoration of the lost knowledge.

Yeats was in a sense immensely optimistic, in contrast, for example, with his younger contemporary T. S. Eliot; who, with David Jones, was perhaps the last major poet of Christendom writing in the English language. Both these poets saw only the advent of a new Dark Age and were deeply pessimistic; whereas Yeats's scale was so much vaster that he was able to envisage a time when "all things run / On that unfashionable gyre again"— the gyre which had produced, in former times, "workman, noble and saint", human types of a spiritually oriented culture. And even in academic circles Yeats's very great work, *A Vision*, is now beginning to be taken seriously; not, I hope (as with too many modern academic studies of Blake) in order to de-fuse and neutralize his too dangerous prophecies.

To thus call in question the value of secular humanist scholarship, and even of its motives, in these fields is not a matter of mere personal opinion, mine and a few others', against theirs: it is a question of urgency in a far larger context. And, incidentally Mrs. Yeats thought so too; I never met Yeats himself, but Mrs. Yeats invited me to visit her house in Palmerston Road, in Dublin, in order to see Yeats's marginalia in his Blake library. She left me with the books for some time and then she came to sit with me. In one hand she carried a Cona coffee machine, and in the other a hot water bottle, which she put behind her back; so, obviously, she came prepared for a long conversation, which indeed we had. When I left she pointed to a pile of books, quite a high pile of books, all by Yeats critics, in the hall and asked me if I would like any of them. I looked at them and said, "No, frankly, I wouldn't like any of them"; what I would like, I said, was an *anenome pulsatilla* from Mrs. Yeats's garden—she was clearly a skilled and discriminating gardener. She gave me, therefore, the *anenome pulsatilla*, which I still have, pressed between the pages of my copy of Blake's *Book of Thel*, where that flower, associated with the archaic myth of Venus and Adonis, is represented by Blake as an emblem of the mysteries of the death and rebirth of the soul. That flower

belonged to the "sacred grammar" of the language shared by Blake and Yeats, inherited from the most ancient traditions of Western culture. As for the books in the hall, "W. B. Y. would not have had the slightest idea what they were talking about" was Mrs. Yeats's comment.

You cannot understand a great thinker (and poetry such as Yeats's is the supreme expression of spiritual knowledge and metaphysical thought) if you do not understand his premises, if you are totally ignorant of the language of symbols which he speaks, of the traditional sources upon which he draws; a language worldwide and universal, lucid to those who possess and are prepared to discover that knowledge, but for ever obscure to those who do not. And, of course, Blake's sources, Yeats's sources, still remain to a great extent an excluded knowledge. The study of magic, of alchemy, of theosophy, of psychical research; even the study of the metaphysics and theology of Plotinus, indeed of Plato himself; of Egyptology, in our own decade, in the sense of Schwaller de Lubicz's work —in the academic world these things are simply not knowledge at all. But for Blake they were knowledge, for Coleridge they were knowledge, for C. G. Jung they were knowledge; and for Yeats they were knowledge. And at Lindisfarne also they are, thank God, knowledge.

Waste Land, Holy Land

KATHLEEN RAINE

The British Academy
Warton Lecture on English Poetry
Read 8 December 1976

You have done me the honour of inviting me to give the Warton Lecture for 1976; and since I am a poet I must conclude that it is as a poet that you wish me to speak; not from learned sources but from my own experience of the literary scene as one of the generation who emerged from childhood in the mid-twenties.

Yeats wrote, before the First World War, of 'the rise of soul against intellect, now beginning in the world'. Subsequent history, and literary history, may not seem to support his prophecy; there is little soul and much intellectual arrogance in our world. Yet the voice of the greatest of poets is always prophetic, and Yeats's vision embraced a time-scale far beyond those superficial waves and wavelets of fashion upon the ebb and flow of a greater tide. His younger contemporaries, both in this country and in America, who because they reflected current ideologies thought they understood the direction of history better than Yeats did, ridiculed the great poet's preoccupation with that whole range of knowledge belonging to the soul and its nature.

Auden accused Yeats of not having a sympathetic attitude towards the most progressive thought of his time; by which he presumably meant (I quote) 'the social struggle toward a greater equality' which 'has been accompanied by a growing intellectual acceptance of the scientific method and the steady conquest of irrational superstition'. (The Public *v.* the Late Mr. William Butler Yeats, *Partisan Review,* Spring 1939.) But scientific method has not proved so universal a way to knowledge as Auden's generation had thought; reformist ideologies have been seen to fail; while the transforming power of the words of our century's supreme 'singing-master of the soul' continues to work towards the fulfilment of his prophecy.

It seems to me a very short time since I was myself a young and most obscure poet caught up in that war; not as a combatant but as a fugitive. Now I surprisingly find myself old, looking back on it all, and wondering about the issue of that battle. And it may be that my time has come to turn back the pages of my own book of life, and tell you what it was like to be of the soul's party at that time when intellect—rational, scientific intellect—held the field. I am no victor; at best a survivor; but since the story of those years has been told so often in terms of the then (and still now) current values, it should perhaps be known that there were some who did not assent to those values and who would tell the story differently.

I have chosen the title, *Waste Land, Holy Land* because these are the terms in which I now see the struggle that was taking place. T. S. Eliot, the other major poet of my time has once and for ever described the Waste Land of the modern world; that profane world in which the soul can only suffer exile. For the soul is, as Edgar Allen

Poe understood, native of another country:

> *Lo! in yon brilliant window-niche*
> *How statue-like I see thee stand,*
> *The agate lamp within thy hand!*
> *Ah, Psyche, from the regions which*
> *Are Holy-Land!*
>   *(To Helen)*

It was T. S. Eliot who gave its true name to our time and place: the Waste Land. His judgement had nothing to do with politics, with W. H. Auden's social struggle; Eliot's truth was the truth of the soul, unable to endure a world in which many would, before the two world wars, have seen a picture of prosperity. He declared our world waste and his great poem is a lamentation because life in that country has withered at the roots. I first read a poem by T. S. Eliot in a magazine I picked up by chance on the table of a provincial newspaper—*The Criterion*. I was at that time (1926) so ignorant as never to have heard his name and I therefore had, as a first-year undergraduate, the pleasure of discovering him for myself; for the impact was instantaneous and tremendous. Here, I felt—and how many others felt as I did— is a voice that speaks the unspoken, the nameless disquiet in which I, as a member of my generation, found myself. That generation (and we were fortunate) had been brought up on Shakespeare and the Romantic poets and Palgrave's *Golden Treasury*; 'modern' poetry was the Georgian poets who wrote of rural life; Walter de la Mare, and Gilbert Murray's translations of the Greek drama. Going up to Cambridge in the mid 1920s as a student of natural sciences I found the ground cut from beneath me; those old assumptions made by the Romantic poets, for whom poetry was the natural speech of the soul, withered in the light of logical positivism, dialectical materialism, and the prestigious 'science' of the Cavendish Laboratory, which recognized no soul at all. Eliot's

poems explored with undeniable truth the state of being which must, without that fiction or reality which the age had disallowed, pass for the real world. This was the region, this the soil, the clime my generation must inhabit; the romantic dream had failed and we found ourselves imprisoned in a profane and soulless reality no poet had as yet explored.

Here I must say that I am not venturing to attempt a 'criticism' of Eliot's poetry nor an evaluation of it; only I am recalling the impact of that poetry upon myself and others of my generation of *entre deux guerres*. Those who read his poetry now may find in it more than we did, read it more accurately or in truer perspective; but that first impact is irrecoverable. In words of Dantesque gravity Eliot's poetry gave words to an experience whose truth found its echo in our own condition. We did not read his poems in any perspective at all: rather we were in them, ourselves figures in the sad procession of Eliot's London, that 'unreal city' in whose unreality lay its terrible reality. We knew that city by participation, knew it too well to criticize or evaluate. We knew the Thames whence Spenser's nymphs had departed, the rat-infested shore and the gasworks. Of the glory of Cleopatra's barge or Gloriana's there remained only the luxury of Bond Street. When Goldsmith's 'lovely woman stoops to folly' it matters; there is Mr. Primrose to seek his fallen daughter and bring her home; but now, the joyless seduction of a tired typist in her transient furnished room matters neither to herself nor to anyone else. Instead of the pride of work there is the joyless procession of wage-earners over London Bridge and the echo of Dante's 'I had not thought death had undone so many'. Indeed we may often have misunderstood the poet whose words we borrowed as a kind of magical incantation to help us to bring under control the situation of our own lives. For my generation had not yet become accustomed to a soulless world and continued to mourn an absence no longer felt—or no longer consciously felt—by the generation who succeeded us. I remember chanting to myself from *Ash Wednesday* the words 'Because I do not hope to turn again / Because I do not hope / Because I do not hope to turn'. Eliot's words lent a kind of valedictory dignity to the turning away from a lost Paradise we still remembered, the halting rhythms of his free verse kept pace with our own knowledge that the 'viewless wings of poesy' were now only 'vans to beat the air'.

Eliot's is the voice of the suffering soul which cannot endure a world stripped of every sanctity by those very ideologies adhered to by most of those who at that time acclaimed him: I remember the shocked surprise with which we learned that Eliot was a Christian. He described our world within the context of the Christian religion, but we saw his burning indictment merely as true to life.

Psyche is in exile, yet again and again the poet invokes her suffering or absent figure; she is the 'Lady of silences, Calm and distressed' who is the 'End of the endless / Journey to no end'; the weeping garden girl who weaves the sunlight in her her hair; the 'silent sister veiled in white and blue'; she is Marina, the absent daughter whose return brings peace, and whose very name suggests the long sea-wandering years of separation. Who are all these feminine figures, or the 'Lady whose shrine stands on the promontory' but Poe's Psyche with her inextinguishable lamp whose country is the holy land, the 'garden where all loves end', our native Eden now withered into the waste land by her absence? Eliot's poetry gave utterance to the suffering of a profane society which had no place for the soul to whom alone belong the shrine, the garden and the end of every journey.

Already in *The Love Song of J. Alfred Prufrock* the poet has entered the Waste Land; the poem is prefaced by a passage from the *Inferno* and there immediately follows an invitation to another descent:

> Let us go, then, you and I
> When the evening is spread out against
>   the sky
> Like a patient etherised upon a table;
> Let us go, through certain half-deserted
>   street,
> The muttering retreats
> Of restless nights in one-night cheap
>   hotels
> And sawdust restaurants with oyster-
>   shells:
> Streets that follow like a tedious
>   argument
> Of insidious intent
> To lead you to an overwhelming
>   question...

We have entered the joyless realm and the landscape is familiar. Every image suggests sickness and despair; the evening sky, no longer Hopkins's 'dappled-with-damson-west' charged with the 'grandeur of God', can anaesthetize but cannot heal; it is passively 'spread out', the sickness of the patient 'etherised' as for an operation of perhaps fatal outcome transferred to the sky itself since place and state are one and indivisible. The streets are 'half-deserted' as if life has ebbed from them. Instead of home-coming we are reminded of the impermanence of the houses. St. Teresa likened life to a night in a bad inn; and here there are 'one-night cheap hotels' where the 'sleep' of life is restless and haunted by 'muttering' (whose? It can only be our own). We are not led to any solution, but towards an 'overwhelming question':

> Oh, do not ask, 'What is it?'
> Let us go and make our visit.

J. Alfred Prufrock's land is waste because,

in search of love (for the poem is called a love song) or perhaps because, like that legendary knight, he does not know the question or does not dare to ask it, of the Holy Grail, that sacred presence that appears in this world and yet belongs also to another. In the trivial world in which he is trapped the question cannot be asked nor the answer is told. Useless to say

> ...'I am Lazarus, come from the dead,
> Come back to tell you all, I shall tell
>   you all'—
> If one, settling a pillow by her head,
>   Should say:'That is not what I meant
>   at all.
>   That is not it at all...'

Prufrock also dreams, but in those dreams he can find nothing to help him in waking life, to which he must return as to a death:

> We have lingered in the chambers of
>   the sea
> By sea-girls wreathed with seaweed
>   red and brown
> Till human voices wake us, and we
>   drown.

The world of his dreams is cut off from his waking life as utterly as Lazarus's experience beyond the grave; and perhaps these realms are the same, being regions of the inner life, of the timeless, which has no longer any place in, or way of access to the world where men and women meet one another only on a level of triviality, where there is only the all-consuming passage of time: 'There will be time, there will be time', Prufrock says; but for him time is not as for Blake, 'the mercy of eternity'; it brings only old age and death: 'I grow old, I grow old' is the form of Prufrock's despair.

The city, being man's creation, is a more immediate reflection of the spiritual condition of a civilization than is 'nature'; yet nature too can be a waste land, reflecting the inner desert. Edwin Muir's poem *The Cloud* describes the profanation of the arcadian image of the countryman tilling his fields by the teaching that 'God is dead' propagated by the Marxist variant of our Western materialism. The poet and his wife were driving through country roads in Czechoslovakia to attend a Communist propaganda lecture:

> At a sudden turn we saw
> A young man harrowing, hidden
>   in dust, he seemed
> A prisoner walking in a moving cloud
> Made by himself for his own purposes;
> And there he grew and was as if exalted
> To more than man, but not, not glorified:
> A pillar of dust moving in dust: no more
> The bushes by the roadside were
>   encrusted
> With a hard sheath of dust.
> We looked and wondered; the dry
>   cloud moved on
> With its interior image.

Coming away from the lecture which exalted the peasant and his toil while denying in him the divine image,

> ...we longed for light to break
> And show that his face was the
>   face once broken in Eden,
> Beloved, world-without-end lamented
>   face
> And not a blindfold mask on a pillar
>   of dust.

What Edwin Muir felt was an absence of something that should have been there; for Eden is man's native place, or condition and so is Eliot's waste land haunted by an absence, precisely, of the holy; of whose sanctuaries he gave us so many symbols, especially in his later poems. Their placing, like high lights in a dark picture, is all important: Little Gidding, the place where prayers have been said; the Garden with its pool that fills with light; or any

..intersection of the timeless moment
Is England and nowhere. Never
and always.
   (Little Gidding)

It is we who consecrate or desecrate; and cities also have been holy; Jerusalem is the very type of the image of man's inner heaven realized on earth; and Yeats's Holy City of Byzantium in which 'religious, aesthetic and practical life were one...and this vision, this proclamation of their invisible master' the vision of a whole people. Eliot discerned in our world an absence—of all things the hardest to discern, still harder to identify. The death of God, the death of the soul—name as we will the withdrawal of the inner vision from the outer world—lays waste the earth. Eliot situated the profane world in that place in the soul's order of values to which it belongs—in the hells, the kingdom cut off from life.

To the talented group of writers who followed Eliot Psyche's country was not in question. Auden and Day-Lewis and their friends were concerned with the political and economic reform of modern industrial society and the 'social struggle towards a greater equality'. One might ask, 'equality to what?' To Muir's 'blind mask in a pillar of dust' or the traditional Christian 'image of God?' These poets were indeed moralists, and initially of Marxist politics and the Marxist view of man, though Auden later became a Christian, preaching tolerance and charity towards fallen humanity in a fallen world. They no less than Eliot were concerned with the modern urban landscape but with the object of arousing the slumbering political conscience. Their concern was neither to illuminate the drab with reconciling beauty (as James Joyce had re-created Dublin in the light of imagination, humour, love, and acceptance); nor, like Eliot, to voice the protest of the soul in exile. Utopia, not the Kingdom

of Heaven, was their goal; and their work was immediately successful with a generation of waste-landers for whom the outer world had come to seem the whole world. Auden was not concerned with an absence, nor with Prufrock's 'overwhelming question', nor with the shrines and sanctuaries of the soul; rather his object was to focus our attention upon the time-world whose signs and symptoms he so brilliantly read. The world is sick—yes—but whereas Eliot had understood that the remedy is reconsecration, for the poets who succeeded him it was social reform. Fear, horror, guilt, shock, cancer, the grave, jump out of Auden's early poems to startle the reader into repentance like devils in a morality play, against a scene of hard-edged machines—aircraft, and 'the helmeted airman', plate-glass, 'silted harbours, derelict works', arterial roads, fast cars, 'the cigarette-end smouldering on the border.' He involves his reader by the skillful placing of the definite article, implying that we know that world as well as he does: not '*a* helmeted airman' or '*a* Sport Hotel' or '*an* infected sinus' but 'the'—the one we know, the one in which we secretly or guiltily participate: '*Those* handsome and diseased youngsters'; '*that* distant afternoon...they gave the prizes to the ruined boys.' He drives home the imputation of guilt, the inescapable implication in the public world:

You cannot get away, then, no,
Not though you pack to leave within
* an hour,*
Escape humming down arterial roads.

When I first read these poems I did not feel myself to be one of the 'we' Auden sought to mobilize, the 'us' of 'our time' with its shared world of the documentary film and the news bulletin, a world everywhere permeable to the mass media and a collectivity from which no distance can any longer separate us, the dance-band at the Sport Hotel

> *Relayed elsewhere to farmers and*
> *their dogs*
> *Sitting in kitchens in the stormy fens.*
> ('*Consider This and in our time*')

His appeal to a supposedly—and within its own terms a really shared contemporary scene, with its well-placed allusions to Nijinski and Diaghilev (gently cajoling our snobbery), to the van der Lubbe trial and Churchill and Hitler and the rest—why did I not feel the intended response, 'Yes, this is the real world, scene of our actions and our moral choice?' For Auden was a most persuasive moralist—his tone is positively evangelical, full of imperatives—'watch', 'consider', 'summon', 'mobilize', 'it is later than you think'.

Now I can see more clearly than anyone noticed at the time the sleight-of-hand Auden practised on his readers. He sought to cut off the soul from any retreat into those inner sanctuaries where under social conditions of every kind men and women have found refuge and another reality. It seemed to me that Auden, that man of impressive worldly wisdom, and his 'we' sought to close the escape routes and to round us up like a flock of sheep to be driven into his pen, away from that inner country that is everyone's priceless and unpurchased birthright, the imaginative ground we each inhabit. If it can be said that dreamers have too little sense of political realities, too little desire for social change, can it not also be said that political and social unrest afflicts not so much the poor and the ignorant but above all those who have, by our modern ideologies, been driven out of these inner sanctuaries, be these religious shrines or places of dreams? Eliot saw that our profane society was a hell precisely because cut off from that ground; the succeeding generation thought, like Milton's fallen angels, that the 'unreal city' could be made tolerable—could be made Utopia—by social reform.

In this sleight-of-hand Auden was not so much the creator as one expression of the mentality of his time; for current ideologies, and notably Marxism, assume that our humanity belongs totally to the outer world their power-structures can control, that we are economic and social beings only, that our whole environment is comprised within the daily scene. This assumption totally neglects that other half of life in which every individual is free to turn aside into a secret and inviolable universe entirely inaccessible to their collective imperatives.

Again let me disclaim any intention of attempting a critique of Auden's poetry; I am merely describing my own response to that school of writers. Some would consider it the first duty of the poet to be politically 'engaged'; others might reply that poltical change can improve the human condition only in very limited ways; while poetry and the other arts, by building for the soul invisible sanctuaries and regions of contemplation, by exploring and extending the scope of our humanity, from Dante's beatitude to his hells, from Shakespeare's Forest of Arden to Lear's heath, has created—that it is its especial virtue that it can so create, at all times and in all places—areas of inner freedom that we can, and do, inhabit, however circumscribed our outer conditions may be. The fallacy that man lives by bread alone has never been more prevalent than in this century. I did not choose to exchange my inner worlds for Auden's hard-edged reality; if a world may be called real which curtails our humanity of half its realm. Had not Eliot, for that very reason, called the same city 'unreal'?

Believing as I do that poetry is in its proper nature the language of the soul; that its proper function is to create for us images of an inner order all share, to open into every present those secret doors, those ways in; to consecrate and redeem for every generation some parcel of the surrounding waste, I cannot feel that those poets of the thirties, brilliantly and admirably as they may have performed some other necessary social role, were fulfilling the proper and vital task of the poet. Genius, Yeats said, is a crisis which joins for certain moments the sleeping and the waking mind. Only at such moments are we fully human, fully ourselves; and for what else does the poem, the work of art, exist, if not to bring about this union?

Auden was, I think, deeply suspicious of —perhaps feared—the 'other' mind whence comes inspiration. We clashed, I remember, over Blake, when at a party in New York, at the time when I was giving a series of lectures on Blake in Washington, Auden challenged me to admit that Blake was, when all is said and done, 'dotty'. He could never have responded to the declared purpose of our great prophet,

> ...I rest not from my great task!
> To open the Eternal Worlds, to open
>   the Immortal eyes
> Of Man inwards into the Worlds
>   of Thought, into Eternity
> Ever expanding in the Bosom of God,
>   the Human Imagination.
>   (*Jerusalem*, Plate 51.17.20)

Because Eliot and Auden described the same modern urban scene in the same sharply defined images of contemporary situations, the two poets were often compared when they ought rather to have been contrasted. Eliot's London is closer to Blake's, whose 'streets are ideas of Imagination' than to Auden's well-photographed documentary world. Yet even Yeats failed to distinguish, in Eliot's early poems, between the image and its intent. In his much criticized Introduction to the *Oxford Book of English Verse*, he wrote that 'Eliot has produced his great effect upon his generation because he described men and women that get out of bed or into it from mere habit; in describing this life that has

lost heart his own art seems grey, cold, dry'. Yeats made the common mistake of taking Eliot's realistic images at their face value; he if any poet should have taken note of those bright shafts of illumination from another dimension—those clues that tell us that Eliot was at all times describing the actual in terms of the absent; for the hells are such precisely in terms of that from which they are absent; as no poet since Dante has understood more profoundly than did Eliot. While 'Ape-neck Sweeney', type of the totally profane man for whom life is just three things, 'birth, and copulation, and death' could coldly watch the hysteria of the prostitute whose human face is no more than

> *This withered root of knots of hair*
> *Slitted below and gashed with eyes,*
> *This oval O cropped out with teeth*

Eliot reminds us of the unnoticed wisteria by the window behind his 'golden grin'; or that

> *The nightingales are singing near*
> *The Convent of the Sacred Heart.*

The nightingale is Keats's 'immortal bird', type of that music heard by all successive generations; Eliot's 'Convent of the Sacred Heart' the sanctuary of the love that Sweeney profanes.

Yeats made his anthology before 1935; before Eliot had written his Four Quartets. But even then he should have heeded those images whose function is to locate, to identify, to comment upon, the action: the Convent of the Sacred Heart; the weeping girl with her arms full of flowers; 'the lost lilac and the lost sea voices'; all these are things that should be and are not: illuminations of the sacred.

Auden and Day-Lewis in forcing us to confront the social evils of our time shifted the ground of conscience from the inner to the outer world; and many of us felt that we had no answer to give, at that time, to these poltical poets. Not so Yeats; who, though he read their work, he says, with 'some excitement', saw that 'Communism is their *Deus ex Machina*, their Santa Claus, their happy ending, but speaking as a poet I prefer tragedy to tragicomedy'. In other words, he is accusing *them* of being the escapists. 'It was easier to look at suffering if you had somebody to blame for it, some remedy in mind', he wrote. Tragedy comes from within; politics is tragicomic in so far as disaster can at any point be averted by manipulation of outer circumstances. Yeats, an old man of long experience of politics, could say to these young poets who sought to make the good and evil of our inner experience seem less 'real' than social ills, 'No matter how great a reformer's energy a still greater is required to face, all activities expended in vain, the unreformed.' The force of these words, largely unheeded at the time, is now inescapable: the political reformer may alter circumstances; poetry and the other arts can change what we inwardly are.

Auden—as is apparent in his mistrust of Blake and his 'eternal worlds', mistrusted and feared what comes from the imagination, from beyond reason's little conquered territory. It is characteristic of him that in the *Sea and the Mirror* he should have treated Ariel as a suspect figure: Prospero would miss him, with his flights of fancy and indeed his insights—Auden allows him these—but the balance falls on the side of disillusionment, which is presented as the 'real' with which all the characters must come to terms. Never has poet so extolled the light of common day. As the ship sails away from the enchanted island, Prospero speaks:

> ...Alonso's heaviness
> Is lost; and weak Sebastian will
>   be patient
> In future with his slothful conscience
>   —after all, it pays.

> Stephano is contracted to his belly,
>   a minor
> But a prosperous kingdom. Stale
>   Trinculo receives
> Gratis, a whole fresh repertoire of
>   stories, and
> Our younger generation its independent
>   joy.
> Their eyes are big and blue with love;
>   its lighting
> Makes even us look new; yes, today
>   it all looks so easy.
> Will Ferdinand be as fond of his
>   Miranda
> Familiar as a stocking? Will Miranda
>   who is
> No longer a silly lovesick little goose,
> When Ferdinand and his brave world
>   are her profession,
> Go into raptures over existing at all?
> Probably I overrate the difficulties;
> Just the same, I am very glad
>   I shall never
> Be twenty and have to go through
>   that business again,
> The hours of fuss and fury, the
>   conceit, the expense.

So all that enhances life, all that lifts us, albeit momentarily, beyond our everyday selves, is illusory and silly; we must settle down to be ordinary, to be tolerant, and to die. The young lovers have not seen a momentary vision of the gods who move our lives: they are deluded—'our younger generation' who will know better when they are our age. Their eyes are 'big and blue' (the denigration is implicit) with love; to them sacramental (and the Church after all is on their side) which Prospero now calls 'that business' with even an implication of 'the expense of spirit in a waste of shame'. Miranda as a 'stocking'—an inhuman, indeed a shocking image—is more real than the Miranda who sees the whole world renewed in her own Paradisal vision; redemptive, as Eliot in his own comparable figure of Marina implies, to that world itself. Auden would say that Shakespeare, after all, made Prospero bury his magic wand and return to the world; but did he mean those who had visited the Island to forget it? Or is not that Island rather a symbol of the Platonic 'other' world from which the soul descends into ours, 'not in entire forgetfulness'? Was not that island to remain the rectifying vision of those who remember it? Is it not precisely the task of the poet to ensure that we do not cease to 'go into raptures over existing at all' when young love is only a memory?

In justice to Auden we must remember that he did write of all-too-human love with great compassion. His love-poem with the opening lines,

Lay your sleeping head, my love,
Human on my faithless arm

is a most moving expression of love as it must be for those who have forgotten. But without the archetype, the image of the soul that Eliot never relinquished, the 'Lady of Silences', the quasi-divine 'Lady whose shrine stands on the promontory', the all-too-human must lose its dignity and that sacred core which, as Conrad said, is at the heart of every human love. Eliot knew, perhaps better than Auden himself, the waste land of human love when that sacred core has been lost: Sweeney is a figure that is too nakedly hellish for any humanist to confront.

Had Yeats made his anthology ten years later he would have found poets more after his own heart than Auden and his circle; poets in whom he might have seen the beginnings of the fulfilment of his own prophecy of the 'rise of soul against intellect'. It was with relief that readers who had, obscurely if not consciously, failed to find imaginative sustenance in Auden's kind of poetry turned to Dylan Thomas whose earthly paradise is made of the simple elements of a country childhood. The word 'holy'—a word that had not been found in poetry for many years—is characteristic of

him; all is praise and celebration. What symptoms of political and economic sickness Auden might have seen no less in the valleys of Wales than in the Pennines it is easy to imagine: Dylan Thomas found holy land. The people of Milkwood live in their dreams, good and bad, their inner lives woven and interwoven with the outer life of their village, incorrigibly oblivious to all collectivizing propaganda.

Auden looked for the steady conquest of the irrational: Vernon Watkins, from his early *Ballad of the Mari Lwyd* and throughout his work, reminds us that the house of life stands in a great surrounding darkness that is also native to us; whose voices speak to us from a timeless world with a strange oracular tongue, reminding us of what we are. The dead are not, for him, non-existent: they are a dimension of ourselves, their communications, as for Eliot, 'tongued with fire / Beyond the language of the living'. Our universe is not the world of politician and newscaster but of the soul's history.

It may be objected that, whereas T. S. Eliot and Auden were aware of the predicament of urban mankind, these Welsh poets knew nothing of the urban environment with its consequent ideologies which has thrown so many into a state of spiritual alienation. One poet—too little known—did notably seek to rediscover the holy land in the waste land.

David Gascoyne understood that it is man-made false values and sick states of mind which alone obscure the holy land everywhere and always present. So with the 'nondescript terrain' of *The Gravel-Pit Field*, 'a stretch of scuffy pock-marked waste' that 'sprawls laggardly its acres till/ They touch a raw brick-villa'd rim'. Seen with the eye of vision

...each abandoned snail-shell strewn
Among these blotched dock-leaves
might seem
In the pure ray shed by the loss

Of all man-measured value, like
Some priceless pearl-enamelled toy
Cushioned on a green silk under glass.

He beholds the apotheosis of this waste land; freed from utilitarian or sociological values we may project upon it, even such a field in its 'extreme abasement' is seen in another light as

Between this world and the beyond,
A tabernacle where one stands
As though within the empty space
Round which revolves the Sage's wheel.

Eliot, in one of his *Preludes*, tells of walking at night in London streets aware of the sleepers who will presently and tragically awake

Impatient to assume the world.

The poet is moved by the mystery of their sleep,

. .moved by fancies that are curled
Around these images, and cling:
The notion of some infinitely gentle,
Infinitely suffering thing.

David Gascoyne's *Night Thoughts* is London's nocturne; a phantasmagoria of illusion and loneliness, in which this poet, not focused upon the harsh realities of day, reflects: 'The boundaries of the senses are not often clearly realised. The Infra and the Ultra are fields easily forgotten. Out of hearing stays unthought-of; out of sight is out of mind. And yet, how haunted we are.' He 'half hopes to overhear—that haunted thing.' It is through this nameless 'being' that 'We are closer to one another than we realise. Let us remember one another at night, even though we do not know each other's names.' The poet calls us together not in the harsh light of waking day, but in participation of the inner, hidden regions of the sleeping mind.

Day-Lewis in his poem *The Flight* attempted to make a specifically machine-age poem (doubtless at the time sharing Auden's enthusiasm for science) celebrating the airace and his craft, implicitly setting these beside Achilles and Cuchulain, those bronze-age heroes and their armour. The courage is doubtless the same in our technological age as in any other, but I think the poem fails because some artefacts are so complete an expression of the soulless mentality that conceived them as not to be susceptible of any symbolic imaginative existence otherwise than as symbols of that soullessness. This was the considered view of Eliot's friend the poet and painter David Jones whose poem *In Parenthesis* is at once the epic of modern warfare (his theme is the trenches of the First World War) and a consecration of the most waste of all land, the battlefield. But it was not our modern technology he praised:

I said, Ah! what shall I write?
I enquired up and down.
(He's tricked me before
with his manifold lurking-places.)
I looked for his symbol at the door.
I have looked for a long while
at the textures and contours
I have run a hand over the trivial
intersections.
I have journeyed among the dead forms
causation projects from pillar to pylon.
I have tired the eyes of the mind
regarding the colours and lights
I have felt for His Wounds
in nozzles and containers.
I have wondered for the automatic
devices.
I have tested the inane patterns
without prejudice.
I have been on my guard
not to condemn the unfamiliar.
For it is easy to miss Him
at the turn of a civilization.

I have watched the wheels go round in
case I might see the living creatures like
the appearance of lamps, in case I might
see the Living God projected from the
Machine. I have said to the perfected steel,
be my sister and for the glassy towers I
thought I felt some beginnings of His

creature, but A, a, a, Domine Deus, *my hands found the glazed work unrefined and the terrible crystal a stage-paste...* Eia, Domine Deus

(The Sleeping Lord, 1974)

If David Jones has written an absolutely modern epic of war it is not because he saw modern warfare as unprecedented but because he discerned in the English Tommy in his khaki uniform the timeless figure of the soldier, in modern warfare, the same war that was waged at Troy, or at Badon Hill, or sung in the epic of the Welsh battle of Catraeth or in the Chanson de Roland. If in *In Parenthesis* tin helmet and barbed wire are of a like significance with the Cross and the Crown of Thorns, it is because those who wore them and died upon them share our humanity. Machines may be unprecedented but to the men of the battlefield the 'strange shapes of death' are what they always were. If it has seemed to some that modern warfare is worse than the sacking of Jerusalem by Titus and Vespasian, or the massacre of Drogheda by Cromwell, or the French retreat from Moscow, it is because of the numbers involved; to the individual soldier the situation is neither better nor worse. Death on the battlefield is one of the situations mankind has confronted from time immemorial; and in that situation other ages have been able to find imaginative meaning, however dark. Death, after all, is one of the unchangeable elements of our human existence. Our human range is finite; progress can bring no joy greater than men and women have at all times experienced; nor can there be any situation of unprecedented evil, cruelties and abominations worse than other ages have known. Under whatever political regime—in Utopia itself— our humanity is attuned to a scale of joy and grief which is ever the same. Suffering is immeasurable, as joy also is, in quantitative terms; weapons may be unprecedented but death is not.

In a profane world death is as meaningless as life; and in this respect alone perhaps is modern warfare unprecedented: our wars and our peace alike are waste land. In his great poem David Jones has shown that in our own, as in other ages, the hells are harrowed. Indeed if the worst conceivable situations which our humanity may have to confront lie beyond the scope of poetry, then poetry itself is a mere diversion.

David Jones's battlefield is certainly not a presentation of that 'passive suffering' Yeats said was no theme for poetry. The situation is redeemed by the presence—the imaginative as well as the physical presence—of men in all their poignant physical vulnerability, but also in the dignity of their confrontation. Auden's 'helmeted airman' is not human but a spare part of a machine: we are not shown his face. David Jones's soldiers of the London Welsh Infantry in tin helmet and khaki puttees tell us who they are, bringing with them their own memories and those of their race. Because of their presence the battlefield itself becomes holy ground.

> *This Dai adjusts his slipping shoulder-*
> *straps, wraps close his misfit outsize*
> *greatcoat—he articulates his English*
> *with an alien care.*
> *My fathers were with the Black Prinse*
> *of Wales*
> *at the passion of*
> *the blind Bohemian king.*
> *They served in these fields,*
> *it is in the histories that you can read*
> *it, Coporal—*
> *boys Gower, they were—it is writ*
> *down—yes.*
> *Wot about Methuseleum, Taffy?*
> *I was with Abel when his brother*
> *found him,*
> *under the green tree.*
> *I built a shit-house for Artaxerxes.*
> *I was the spear in Balin's hand*
> *that made waste King Pellam's land.*
> *I took the smooth stones of the brook,*

I was with Saul
playing before him.

In Dai's Boast (which runs to some five or six pages) he tells us who he is; he stands on the everlasting battlefield of the earth in his full human stature and even in the dignity of his human free will, albeit the free will to accept but not to change the event. Wherever man is present the sacramental consecration is possible; even on the battlefield. Perhaps especially on that field, where so much is demanded of men, who often surpass themselves; 'the ''Bugger! Bugger!'' of a man detailed had often about it the ''Fiat! Fiat!'' of the Saints.'

Finally, Edwin Muir, the poet who of all those I have known, most clearly realised that we live in two worlds and that our waking life is rooted in the soul's timeless country. I remember with what gratitude I first listened to him saying so simply all those things I had scarcely allowed myself even to think. But Edwin, for all his quiet gentleness, had a mind that no tide or wind of fashion could deflect from the certainties of his insight. Very early in our acquaintance he asked me if I ever wrote poems from dreams, and I said No. He told me that I should because dream is so important a part of our reality, an aspect of our world and of ourselves. We live in the waking day for little more than half of our time and perhaps even less of our being. There is a life of the night also:

I have been taught by dreams
and fantasies,
Learned from the friendly and the
darker phantoms

—so he wrote in one of his last poems. Again and again he speaks of the knowledge of the night:

The night, the night alone is old
And showed me only what I knew,
Knew, yet never had been told;
A speech that from the darkness grew
Too deep for daily tongues to say,

Archaic dialogue of a few
Upon the sixth or the seventh day.
And shapes too simple for a place
In the day's shrill complexity
Came and were more natural, more
Expected than my father's face
Smiling across the open door.
(Day and Night)

And yet of all his contemporaries it was Edwin Muir who was most directly involved in the political tragedies of Europe before and after the Second World War. He saw at first hand the rise of Nazism in Germany; the disasters that befell Czechoslovakia (he was Director of the British Institute in Prague) first from the German occupation, then following the Communist *coup d'Etat*. But he understood the outer event in terms of the inner, and saw that the worst violations were those upon the soul. None of his many explicitly descriptive poems better expresses the everlasting paradox of aggressor and victim than *The Combat*, written from a dream. The conflict was one he witnessed in the world of his time, but in the dream the emotion is naked; external events are after all but an expression of the eternal conflict within ourselves and is not even history the enactment of our dreams? Over and over again the aggressor, the 'crested animal in his pride' and the victim—'a soft round beast brown as clay' repeat the battle in which the dream-victim is always defeated and yet never destroyed.

Edwin Muir had at one time taken his dreams to a Jungian analyst, but had soon realised—the analyst also—that these visions properly belonged to the domain of the poet; never to be explained, only to be made known. In a poem entitled *The Poet* he writes of the living and hidden source:

What I shall never know
I must make known,
Where traveller never went
Is my domain.

Even Jung's great reverence for the holy land of the psyche fell short of the poet's experience; Plato's 'garden of the Muses' has ever been the poet's source of inspired knowledge; it is the psychologists who are newcomers.

I have spoken of these poets I have known, who were my friends, in an attempt to discover, and in their enduring words to communicate my own belief that poetry is the proper language of the soul; a speech that never ceases to tell those who are in the time-world of a timeless region that lies beyond the reach of intellectual judgements and evaluations. When the frontier of our consciousness is closed we inhabit a waste land to which neither wealth nor culture can impart life, which no social reform can restore. Thus understood poetry is no mere adornment of the everyday scene but a necessary knowledge of our immortal selves. Because this is so I believe that Yeats's prophecy of the 'rise of soul against intellect' must, sooner or later, fulfil itself, since it is a return to the norm, grounded not only in tradition but in the real nature of things. Truth, Yeats wrote—and he meant the truth of the soul, not of the intellect—'can never be discovered, but may be revealed'; as Edwin Muir also understood when he wrote, of Psyche's holy land,

> Look once. But do not hope to find
>   a sentence
> To tell what you have seen. Stop
>   at the colon:
> And set a silence after to speak
>   the word
> That you will always seek and never
>   find,
> Perhaps, if found, the good and
>   beautiful end.
> You will not reach that place.
>   (*Images, I*)

What is Man?

KATHLEEN RAINE

*A Contribution to a Conference
on Education
at Dartington Hall, England
May 1979*

In considering education it is before all else necessary to ask that oldest of questions, "What is man?" We find the question in the Book of Job, who asks, "What is man that thou shouldest magnify him? and that thou shouldest set thine heart upon him?"(vii.17) Job is quoting from a psalm (viii.3) which reminds us of the paradox of human littleness and human greatness:

> *When I consider thy heavens, the work of thy fingers, the moon and the stars, which thou hast ordained; What is man, that thou art mindful of him? and the son of man, that thou visitest him?*
> *For thou hast made him a little lower than the angels, and hast crowned him with glory and honour. Thou madest him to have dominion over the works of thy hands; thou hast put all things under his feet.*

St. Paul quotes this psalm in his Epistle to the Hebrews, in order to present to the Jews, familiar with the scriptures, the new concept of Jesus as the divine humanity incarnate; and all these texts look back finally, to the first chapter of Genesis, where the creation of man is described:

> *So God created man in his own image, in the image of God created he him.* (i.27)

—and the passage goes on to describe the dominion given to man over all living things on the earth.

When Job reminds God of his exaltation of man he does so in bitterness, complaining that man is a creature of dust who goes down to the grave unregarded. Nevertheless the theme which runs through the Bible, from Genesis to the Epistle to the Hebrews, is man as the image of God, bearer of the divine imprint; Jesus, as the Son of Man, is the realization of the first-created humanity, the *anthropos*, as imagined by the Creator before the Fall; which Fall is the result of Adam's "sleep", a loss of consciousness, a "descent", as the Greeks would say, from a spiritual to a natural mode of consciousness, with a consequent self-identification not with the spiritual but with the natural body; which is, as Job complains, a thing of dust.

The Greeks too asked the question, "What is man?"—the riddle of the Sphinx: "What is it that in the morning goes on four legs, at midday on two legs, and in the evening on three legs?"—a bitter evocation of the mortal worm who creeps from helpless infancy, though a brief and infirm prime, to the helplessness of infirm age. Oedipus guessed the riddle and, by implication, acknowledged the truth of the Sphinx's description of man.

This is of course the widely accepted view of mankind in modern secular societies. Week in week out the evolutionists describe natural man on the mass media; the schools assume the finality of the scientific description of reality, including natural man. (Who dares question the infallibility of science—natural knowledge—or its pronouncements?) Thus in our secular society man the mortal worm is, paradoxically, denied the only dignity which properly belongs to us—our spiritual nature—and at the same time proclaimed as the lord of creation. Education of the mortal worm for a brief life on earth is inevitably therefore designed to fit men and women to the performance of tasks concerned with bodily life, tasks more or less skilled, but all alike directed to the production of material goods and the construction and control of machines, also utilized for material ends. Ultimately man becomes, within such an order, a replaceable spare-part in the great machine a materialist society has constructed, with a built-in obsolescence after fifty years or so of efficient functioning. The modern state is a self-perpetuating machine built to last longer than any individual life-time and we like to pretend that the state, or the world super-state, will last for ever—well, nearly for ever, and what difference is there between eternity and a very long time indeed? The world will last our time, we shall not be here at the end; at most we wonder about our grandchildren, but who cares about their own progeny six generations hence? "They are destroyed from morning to evening: they perish for ever without any regarding it." (Job iv.20)

This is the implicit, and sometimes explicit, view of the materialist Western society to which we belong, and it is difficult to remain totally untouched by the evolutionism of materialist society, which recognizes only a material order, with humankind as part of that order—the most complex and "evolved" species which has produced man as the cleverest of the primates, by a process of "natural selection". This process may produce cleverer primates yet and (as many hopefully believe) is bound to do so, because evolution, guided though it is by blind chance, can result only in Utopia. (Utopia, be it said, in the modern sense of the word, as a society in which all temporal mankind's aspirations and desires will be realized. It is questionable whether the Catholic Thomas More expected a society without any spiritual order to have any such result.) In the modern Utopian dream, every disease will be "conquered" and so perhaps will death, and no one will go hungry or unintegrated within the social structure; as for living, our machines will do that for us, thereby freeing us to enjoy this hell of spiritual meaninglessness for as long as we can endure it.

Utopians never give up their myth: the plain evidence goes to show that the English nation (to look no further afield) simply cannot stand it, that the schoolchildren do not want to be trained for the kind of "jobs" that the machines provide, in the technological Utopia where thinking is something computers do, where "the brain" is synonymous with mind and thought. We have even had it claimed that a computer can write poems, and truth to say the examples given were all too like many produced by human beings who conceive themselves in physical terms. Students engage in revolution, destruction making small demands in comparison with the complex programming of the University syllabus; besides satisfying some unformulated and baffled sense of frustration engendered by the secular society. The mass of mankind—the worker-ants—misled by the ever present advertisements which tell us that Utopia is in every packet of this or that, grasp what they can, forever deceived by the trash of the machines which cheats their dreams of realization. Who can blame them that they are dissatisfied? Clever cynics who know about human dreams paint for them those desert-islands, those far shores and clear Paradisal streams, unfelled trees, unbulldozed meadows, un-ravished Eves, that forever elude the pur-chasers of cigarettes and convenience foods, underwear and insurance policies, cos-metics made from slaughtered whales whose rotting carcases stink upon the real shores; and all the celestial omnibuses are driven on oil and coal and steel from Paradise Lost, the tasteless bread and canned vegetables harvested from a waste land where the wild and the bees are sprayed with poison, the rabbits, so popular on children's cot-covers, die of myxomatosis, and as the motorist fancies a tiger in his tank the real tigers of the earth are threatened with extermination. The world has never been more hideous, more uninhabitable, than the world created by an ideology which claims that this world is all, which gives to matter a primacy, an all-importance unknown to other civili-zations. Decidedly the way to Utopia is long and hard for the last of the primates.

If man is indeed what Blake calls the mortal "Worm of sixty winters" and "seventy inches long", born in a night to perish in a night, what can education be? In a world of pure materialism education can only be utilitarian, a training to fit the human spare part for the function it is to perform during its few useful years; after which there is nothing to expect but death, and death is the end, as birth was the beginning of life. The satisfaction of natural appetites is presumed to give the mortal worm, or naked ape, those satisfactions of which we are capable, including music, whose rhythms serve to stimulate or soothe, food and shelter, sensual pleasure, freedom from pain, hunger, cold, or the dis-orientation of those habits to which we are conditioned; "programmed", as it is nowadays called. And so, "distracted from distraction by distraction", as T. S. Eliot wrote of the dwellers in the waste land, we "get by". Drugs can alleviate whatever states of anxiety our souls may cause us,

and there is yet another industry to cater for our inevitable dreams or day-dreams; for these are an as yet unexplained flaw in the perfect adaptation and functioning of mortal life: mankind continues to imagine quite other things.

The Utopian view of humanity is of course untrue; untrue not because the deductions of science concerning natural law are incorrect within their own terms—the great merit of the scientific method is its respect for evidence and, in that sense, for truth—but untrue because the assump-tion, the premise of Western science that nothing exists other than the quantifiable natural world, is false. Consciousness—to take the most obvious thing in the world—cannot, for example, be quantified, cannot be dealt with at all in terms of weight and measure, of those extensions in space or in time which are the only terms proper to material science. Mental and physical enti-ties are incommensurable not because sci-ence has not "as yet" found a way of describing mental events in physical terms but because these belong to distinct orders. In measuring the brain waves of dreamers or of meditators scientists have not come one whit nearer to measuring the dreams or states of consciousness themselves, as such; nor can they ever do so within the terms of their proper field of knowledge. This is no reproach to natural science, which has its own field, and whose account of natural phenomena is impressive indeed —a field which rightly includes man's physical frame, its anatomy, physiology, and place within the natural universe.

But so overwhelmed are we by wave after wave of information about man's nat-ural evolution and affinity with nature on the one side, and on the other medical explanations of whatever concerns the psy-che, that we easily forget that man is *not* merely a clever primate; we forget that the brain is *not* the mind, that consciousness is *not* a property of the sense organs of which it makes use. We forget, in fact, that man is not a species of animal but a new kingdom, as distinct from the animal kingdom as mammals are distinct from rocks. Each kingdom, from the mineral to the vital, from the vital to the animate, from animal consciousness to the human kingdom of the Imagination, is subject to new laws proper to itself. This Teilhard de Chardin has made very clear to our generation, but still has not clearly enough reminded us that mankind, as human (for of course we share the laws of chemistry with the mineral world, the vital physiology with plants, and our bodily senses with the animals) is an invisible kingdom whose world is a mental world, subject to laws proper to itself which do not conform to the categories of time and space, or to any of the laws of "nature". Because this is in reality so, and equally so for atheists as for Christians, for Marxists as for Buddhists, the extreme picture of man as a spare part of his own machines can never altogether come about. We cannot dehumanize ourselves. Whereas our opinions can make us very unhappy and raise in us all kinds of conflicts between what is so and what we opine to be, they cannot alter the reality of what we are. We continue to be human, and insofar as we are human we are spiritual beings.

Western materialism is an unprecedented departure from human culture, as it has existed and developed from the Stone Age to the present time. From the oldest examples of human art we see humankind seeking to express ideas, to discover a mental order; to explore our inner worlds in terms of pantheons of "gods" who personify the qualities of human consciousness, our moods and modes of experience. From the earliest known human records we see humankind creating abstract patterns and forms not found in nature; gods of strange unnatural aspect—the more un-natural the more profoundly "human". Modern Amazonian savages asked Levi-Strauss, that civilized Frenchman, why he and his kind did not paint their faces with abstract patterns in order (like the Amazonians) to affirm their humanity, their difference from the animals around them. They knew what Western anthropologists would seem to have forgotten, that to be human is, precisely, to live our myths, to live according to an inner order which is not natural, which is, in terms of natural law, unnatural. The distortions and deformations of the human face and body, the paintings and tattooings practised by primitives from the land of El Dorado to Borneo to the Congo are supremely, specifically human, being expressions of a mental, an inner world, affirmed in opposition to, in challenge of, in affirmation against, a natural order. The pantheons of more advanced societies are more psychologically complex and subtle explorations of those inner regions of human consciousness. The faimilar gods of Greece—still, in many respects, our own self-knowledge personified—are not mere moods and passions but intellections of great subtlety, related each to certain fields of knowledge. The Orphic theology in all its complexity of hierarchic relationship and causality is unsurpassed as an account of mankind's invisible worlds, a system no less elaborate in its structuring than the scientists' description of the kingdoms of nature. To name only one or two of the most obvious examples of the distinctness of these inner fields, Apollo is the principle of all mental clarity, knowledge of music and number, medicine, the ordering principle that belongs to the enlightened mind, to the rational; the changing moon-goddess belongs to dark knowledge of the blood, to parturition, witchcraft, all kinds of feminine regions of experience. Dionysus is the genius of ecstatic possession by irrational states of consciousness, an exaltation

unknown to the clear reason of Apollo's kingdom; while Ares takes over the warrior when, like the Irish Cuchulain, the battle-warp siezes him, his hair stands on end, his face is distorted with rage and his body filled with the berserk courage the Vikings delighted in, a transport of rage in which the warriors scarcely felt the wounds of battle. To each god his kingdom. In our century these principles or energies of the psyche which materialist science had thought to dismiss as unrealities, or as primitive attempts by mankind to describe the laws of nature'', have been renamed by C.G. Jung, the ''archetypes'' which are as he says, self-portraits of the instincts. Jung was the tireless reminder of our forgetful age that the psyche is real; that it is also most dangerous. It is not from nature that this world stands in danger of destruction, but from the human mind which has invented hydrogen bombs and the ideologies in whose service such weapons may be used. If the most appalling apocalyptic prophecies are realized it will have been ourselves who have brought them about. The author of the Book of Revelation read only the possibilities within the inner worlds of mankind. We are inclined to

read that book as a threat from an arbitrary and cruel (but fortunately, so the scientists reassure us, non-existent) God; but read that terrifying book as the story of inner events within the human psyche reflected— as our thoughts inevitably must be—in the world of history—and we must tremble, not at what ''God'' might do to us, but at what we ourselves have it in us to do to ourselves and to our world. Is not that prophecy of poisoned seas and rivers, of Armageddon, of shelterless refugees, of destruction falling from the skies, already realized, not by some cosmic catastrophe or arbitrary act of ''victimization'', as it is called, of innocent humankind by a demon-god, but by the demons who inhabit the human soul?

All the great religious traditions have been attempts to cultivate the human soul. Our materialist civilization has concerned itself with the well-being of the naked apes, with food and shelter and the learning of the skills necessary to the survival of the body; but every attempt to bring order to the inner worlds, to nourish the specifically human, has gone by default. Not altogether so, of course, for the past is still powerful and two thousand years of Christendom and all the wisdom of the Greek and the Hebrew traditions before that are still with us; or at least with the educated sections of society, who are less at the mercy of current ideologies. Pythagoras continues to impose upon the soul the order of the dia-tonic scale through such music as is still composed according to its laws. Christian art continues to remind us of the celestial hierarchies of angels, of the lives of saints lived in accordance with the laws not of nature but of the spirit; of the Christian myth of the birth of the divine principle into the world of generation, fully manifested in that sublime figure of Christ Pantocrator, the ruler of all, depicted in the dome of every Orthodox basilica; and whose suffer-ing under the world-rulers for whom man is natural man, the armed ape and the togaed ape, the image of the Crucifixion in Western Catholicism has never allowed us to forget. For the struggle to rise from the natural to the human kingdom is hard and endless, and none of us has succeeded so well that we can afford to dismiss the symbol of the Crucifixion, which Utopians would like to banish from their brave new world; which is the hell of the human spirit whose kingdom, as it is said in the Christian Gospel, is ''not of this world''.

Let me remind you that we are still considering the question, ''What is man?'' I have suggested that man is, in truth, not a mortal worm, but a spiritual being, immaterial, immeasurable, who is never born and never dies, because spirit is not bounded or contained within the categories of the material world of time and space, of duration and extension. In this sense we are immortal, eternal, boundless within our own universe. Yet of the kingdom that is truly ours, specifically human, we have realized very little.

Nowadays the term ''human'' has been inverted to the point of signifying precisely what is least human in us, our bodily appetites and their gratification, and all that belongs to natural man; while the study of philosophy, for example, or the practice of some religious asceticism is considered ''inhuman''. Nothing in our ''permissive'' society is held to be more ''human'' than the act of sex; but Alexander the Great—Aristotle's pupil—said that man was never *less* human than in that act. He was not, of course, speaking of love, which is of the soul and has no necessary connection with the sexual instinct. Sex is an animal function, love a human experience. It is all too easy to revert to the animal which we, as humanity, must labour to transcend in order to come into even a small portion of our potential kingdom. The late Dr. Schumacher, who in his last book,

A Guide for the Perplexed, made many things so clear, liked to quote Aquinas's words, ''Even the least knowledge of things superior is of greater value than the most extensive knowledge of things inferior.''

Having, therefore, reminded ourselves that humanity, insofar as we are human, is a kingdom not in nature, ''not of this world'', but an invisible inner universe, let us consider this universe a little more closely.

While every pantheon is a less or more perfect, a more or less crude and simple, or subtly complex representation of the structure of the human inner worlds, certain elements seem to recur and to represent the abiding structure of the psyche. The sphere quadrated by a six-armed cross, or the circle quadrated by a four-armed cross; fourness under many symbols—the four-faced gods of India; the four sons of the Egyptian Harpocrates; Jesus Christ with the four evangelists, the four ''living creatures'' of Ezekiel's fourfold Chariot of God, or the lion, eagle, ox and angel of the Book of Revelation. C. G. Jung in his psychological types has made the Four familiar as the ''functions'' of the human psyche, reason, feeling, sensation and intuition. Blake, basing his symbols upon Ezekiel and St. John, describes the

four "Zoas" or "living creatures" whose conflicts and rebellions form the drama of his Prophetic Books. These Four are in every man; and Blake speaks of the Four Zoas as the four "faces" of the Universal Man; as the four rivers of Paradise; as four "worlds" or "universes"—distinct worlds, each with its own mode of knowledge, distinct and incommensurable, as feeling or intuition with reason, or sensation with the other three. Blake, at the end of the eighteenth century, had already diagnosed what he calls "the sickness of Albion"—that is, of the English national being—as the usurpation by the rational function—Urizen—of the throne and sceptre of supremacy which properly belongs to the imagination, the "human existence itself" and divine anthropos, made in the image of God, which is above the Four. Urizen is the rational mind, basing its deductions upon what Blake calls a "ratio of the five senses", and his creation is scientific materialism. The rational mind is aware of no form of knowledge higher than itself, calling the Imagination "delusion and fancy". This spiritual sickness of the English nation Blake saw typified in those culture-heroes of science, Bacon, Newton and Locke (to whose number others have since been added—Darwin, Huxley, Russell and so on) who share the false premise of all, that "matter", a substance existing apart from the mind which perceives it, is the only ground of the "real". Under the rule of Urizen, feeling becomes no longer a mode of knowledge, but a selfish emotion; while intuition, refusing the rule of Urizen, rebels in vain. Although Blake was well able to argue the case against rationalism in its own terms—and did so most trenchantly—his most powerful weapon was the depiction of man the rationalist, anxious and purblind, unable ever to complete his conquest of the rebellious energies of life; a foolish travesty of God the Father.

Blake describes the "sickness of Albion" under the usurping rule of Urizen as a "deadly sleep", using the Platonic term, which sees unconsciousness, oblivion of the real, forgetfulness of the eternal worlds within, as the mark of the human condition described in the Jewish-Christian tradition as the Fall. Mankind is "fallen", specifically, from a human (imaginative) into a natural mode of consciousness. Thus understood, the Fall has nothing to do with the commission of certain specific "sinful" acts, but is a descent from a higher state of being into a lower, from the Imagination to the natural body; as symbolised, in the Biblical story, by the eating of the apple of sexuality.

Every "revealed" tradition is agreed upon the essential structure of the human psyche, of that invisible inner universe which is the properly human kingdom, from which we have "fallen" into natural life; all holding our present state of consciousness as imperfect in relation to that which we essentially are, and man as first created in the order of "origins", by which a temporal beginning in the sense of the scientific evolutionists is not of course meant, but rather the type, pattern, archetype of the *anthropos*, "made in the image of God", as described in the first chapter of Genesis. The "human", according to tradition, is not, as for our own society, natural man but the archetypal perfect humanity, of whom every average man is a more or less obscured and distorted image. Our own secular society has sought to make everyone happy by taking as the norm "fallen" man, Plato's dwellers in the Cave; but flattery of our fallen, or forgetful condition can only superficially and briefly deceive us into believing that all is well, that we are all we should be, since each of us carries within ourselves, however, obscured, the image of the *anthropos*, called by the Hindus the Self, by the Buddhists the

Buddha-nature, by the Jews Adam Kadmon, by the Christians Jesus the Christ, by Blake the Divine Humanity. Jung has chosen to use the Indian term, the Self (spelt with a capital in distinction from the individual selfhood, or empirical ego) as being perhaps the least localised name by which the God Within can be described and identified. The goal of human life is the total realization and attainment in our lives of this archetypal humanity, our true spiritual identity.

This is a goal few have attained. The Buddhist world holds that Prince Siddhartha attained perfect enlightenment; Christians believe that Jesus was the Christ, fully incarnating the archetypal first-created Son of God. The Hindu tradition holds that there have been several revelations of the divinity in human form; that whenever the world has fallen into spiritual darkness a new revelation of the divine Person has again made known to us our own forgotten reality. All traditions are agreed that the divine humanity, although the type of all humnaity, has scarcely ever been realized: for the Christian world, once only; for the Jews, not yet but someday; no religious tradition flatters us, as do the Utopians, by allowing us to believe that we come within reach, or barely within apprehension, of that which we essentially are. Human perfection is something scarcely ever attained; few attain enlightnement, few are saints. One of the most deplorable features of the secular West is the universal complacency of a mankind often barely human at all, in properly human terms. Many ''primitive'' races—many American Indians, or the illiterate country people still to be found here and there in the West of Ireland or of Scotland—live upon a higher and more properly human level than the sophisticated products of our technological culture. I do not doubt that many powerful Commissars could learn

much of the real nature of humanity from village grandmothers with shawls over their heads and a corner of icons; icons which are, by definition, depictions of invisible spiritual essences. You find their depictions in the interior of any Orthodox church—the Mother of God, the Pantocrator, angels, saints—or in Italy's pre-Renaissance basilicas—in the Church of Saint Francis at Assisi, where in the episodes of the saint's life Giotto has depicted are all of them spiritual events—dreams, visions, the casting out of demons, the beholding of the eternal Christ. In the secular world the facts that make up our news—the events narrated as biography or as fiction—are all of the natural order; how few belong to this human order, which we of the West have so deeply betrayed.

The theme of this conference is education: need I say more? In order to ''educate'' a human being it is first necessary to answer that old question, ''What is man?'' Are we to process, to condition, to ''form'', to ''brainwash'' natural mankind to fit human beings for a longer or shorter life-span in the natural world and the performance of more or less skilled tasks in the great mechanism? Or ought we not rather to consider man's invisible kingdom, the boundless interior regions we inhabit, the almost unguessed, undiscerned spiritual regions within us, so close to childhood, but later only to be attained through aspirations and disciplines which have little to do with the amassing of facts or the learning of technical skills which passes for education in our secular society?

Blake called the Divine Humanity, the imprinted archetype, the Imagination. Imagination, he said, is ''the true man'', the unifying life of which the Four are the faculties, the instruments. Whereas the soul, with its fourfold universe, is individual, the Imagination is universal—the universal Self alike in all. The word Imagination suggests, in common parlance, the arts; and insofar as, in a normal society, music, painting, poetry and architecture are depictions of mankind's inner worlds, the proper language of the soul, this is true; for whereas science measures the natural world, the arts alone can depict the inner worlds. Blake called music, painting and poetry "man's three ways of conversing with Paradise which the Flood did not sweep away"—the "flood of the five senses" in which materialism drowns and submerges the world of the Imagination. Yeats, writing of the soul's country, also saw the arts as its proper expression; we can only know its invisible nature through those forms in which it is embodied:

> Nor is there singing school but studying
> Monuments of its own magnificence.

How else can we know of those inner invisible forms otherwise than in their expression, their "monuments"? In the same poem Yeats renounces natural forms; he is speaking still of the forms of art:

> Once out of nature I shall never take
> My bodily form from any natural thing,
> But such a form as Grecian goldsmiths
>   make
> Of hammered gold and gold
>   enamelling.

He is thinking of Byzantium, the civilization he held most fully to have expressed a collective human vision of soul's invisible country, "the work of many that seems the work of one", and all in the service of their "invisible Master". That master is, of course, the archetype, the *Anthropos*, the Divine Humanity, the Self, revealing itself through architecture and icon, down to the minute craftsmanship of ivory-carver and goldsmith.

But while it is true that the arts are the proper expression of the inner worlds, of mankind's imaginative self-knowledge, from the caves of Ajanta or Lascaux, to Santa Sophia and Chartres—we must remember that not all that goes by the name of art is an embodiment of inner reality. Plato condemned naturalism in art, the mere imitation of natural behaviour. If the soul and its world—and, above that, the universal Imagination and its order—is not known, how can it be expressed? And that we live in an age of spiritual ignorance is everywhere evident in our art-forms; which are for the most part self-portraits of states of ignorance not of knowledge. Imitative, naturalistic art of the kind fashionable in the nineteenth century was not always without some vision, some reflection of Paradise seen in the forms of nature; we think of Samuel Palmer, of Calvert, Constable, Turner, for whom nature is itself the glass in which Imagination beholds itself; but for many more, realistic depiction is mere trick photography of natural appearances as in the "social realism" of Marxist materialism.

The newer fashions, from abstract impressionism to the present, proclaim art as "self-expression", sometimes glorified by the name "creativity"; American Universities have classes in so-called "creative writing", and in our schools there is endless talk of teaching children to express themselves "creatively". But self-expression is, unfortunately, very far from being an expression of imaginative vision and imaginative knowledge. The final result of this century's guiding principle in the arts of "breaking with the restrictions of the past" in order to be totally "original" has been a school of scribbles whose total originality is total meaninglessness, and of striking uniformity. Such art and such verse expresses only the ignorance of its authors; expresses nothing at all. The only "originality" that has any value is a return to the origin, the lost knowledge of the Imagination.

The art of a secular society has suffered fatally from the identification of "knowledge'' with natural science. It has been forgotten that there can be ''knowledge'', in any precise or universal sense, of the invisible worlds; knowledge no less absolute, no less exact, than science's knowledge of the natural universe. Therefore, whereas we know very well that in order to be a mathematician or a chemist we must study the laws of mathematics or of chemistry, we have forgotten that there is knowledge proper to the soul. It is true that the mathematical and chemical laws of nature are everywhere expressed in the world about us, but we do not for that reason expect our schoolchildren to go and find out for themselves by observation or to practice ''free expression'' in chemistry, or to ''liberate themselves'' from traditional mathematics in order to become original astronomers or physicists. If Einstein's universe is a ''liberation'' from Newton's it presumes prior knowledge of Newton's. We have far too much respect for science to turn it, as we have turned the arts, into a children's play-ground. We cannot expect our children, our ''young'' poets and ''young'' painters to discover for themselves the abiding order of the invisible worlds. Just as those who study mathematics or chemistry or plant morphology respond with recognition to what they are taught, so, far from inhibiting talent and ''creativity'', knowledge of higher things can only awaken a similar response and widen the field of the individual imagination. But we have denied or forgotten that the invisible worlds can be fields of knowledge which can be taught and learned and transmitted and communicated. Other civilizations have taken this to be so as a matter of course. From Indian metaphysics, Platonic theology, Christian doctrine, down to the religiously preserved sacred stories of the most primitive tribes, every race has preserved its own embodiments of a ''revealed'' tradition concerning the inner nature of things, the order of the soul. These theologies, theogonies, sacred rites and tribal myths are not pass-times or self-expression, they are the self-knowledge of the human psyche upon which alone a culture can be based, be that culture simple as that of the Bushman or as metaphysically rich as Vedanta. It is we who are the barbarians—spiritual barbarians, that is—who lack this collective language, this shared knowledge, upon which the goldsmiths of Byzantium, the builders of Chartres, the musicians of the diatonic scale, the painters of Florence, down to Yeats and the poets of the Irish renaissance, drew.

My conclusion, then, is that our materialist secular society, well though it may educate in the natural sciences, altogether fails to educate the human soul, the invisible humanity which is, in Plato's words as well as Blake's, ''the true man''. We are simply not educated in these things which above all make us human. Those who inherit—who have not yet lost, under the cancerous impact of Western ideologies—some metaphysical, religious and iconographic tradition, some language of symbolic images built up throughout a civilization, are fortunate indeed. For the rest of us, all is to be remade; not altogether as if it had never been, for in the relics, in the survivals of the past, we can rediscover lost knowledge, piece by piece reconstructing something, perhaps, which will serve a broken culture without a tradition of its own. Reality is always and everywhere itself; but who shall say whether we can use the language of Christendom, of the Far East, of Islam (the last prophetic revelation,) of Jungian psychology, of Cabbala, of the American Indians? In all the arts there is a confusion of tongues. Blake knew everything except how to find symbolic or linguistic terms to communicate what he knew; he was eclectic in his symbols but orthodox in his Christian theology. Yeats's lifelong labour was to test, to discard or to retain, a great range of symbols and terms drawn from many traditions, Rosicrucian, Neoplatonic, Far Eastern. To recreate a common language for the communication of knowledge of spiritual realities, and of the invisible order of the psyche, is the problem now for any serious artist or poet, as it should be for educators. Yet the problem of language would resolve itself once these worlds were re-opened to our experience for the knowledge itself is primary, the terms—symbols—secondary. This re-discovery, re-learning, is a long hard task—a lifelong task for those who undertake it; yet the most rewarding of all tasks, since it is a work of self-discovery which is at the same time a universal knowledge, "knowledge absolute" as the Vedas claim. So-called "creativity" and "self-expression" will not get us very far. The Grecian goldsmith, the Gothic sculptor, the painter of churches or elaborator of Islamic geometric patterns in a mosque were none of them "expressing themselves" in the modern sense of the term; far less breaking with the past, or being "revolutionary". They were making use of the shared knowledge of a spiritual tradition that illuminates their work, as it illuminated the inner lives of those who participated in its unity of culture.

LENTEN FLOWERS

Primrose, anemone, bluebell, moss
Grow in the kingdom of the cross

And the ash-tree's purple bud
Dresses the spear that sheds his blood.

With the thorns that pierce his brow
Soft encircling petals grow

For in each flower the secret lies
Of the tree that crucifies.

Garden by the water clear
All must die that enter here!

THE PYTHONESS
(For John Hayward)

I am that serpent-haunted cave
Whose navel breeds the fates of men
All wisdom issues from a hole in the earth:
The gods form in my darkness, and dissolve again.

From my blind womb all kingdoms come,
And from my grave seven sleepers prophesy.
No babe unborn but wakens to my dream,
No lover but at last entombed in me shall lie.

I am that feared and longed-for burning place
Where man and phoenix are consumed away,
And from my low polluted bed arise
New sons, new suns, new skies.

ISIS WANDERER

This too is an experience of the soul
The dismembered world that once was the whole god
Whose broken fragments now lie dead.
This passing of reality itself is real.

Gathering under my black cloak the remnants of life
That lie dishonoured among people and places
I search the twofold desert of my solitude,
The outward perished world, and the barren mind.

Once he was present, numinous in the house of the world,
Wearing day like a garment, his beauty manifest
In corn and man as he journeyed down the fertile river.
With love he filled my distances of night.

I trace the contour of his hand fading upon a cloud,
And this his blood flows from a dying soldier's wound.
In broken fields his body is scattered and his limbs lie
Spreadeagled like wrecked fuselage in the sand.

His skull is a dead cathedral, and his crown's rays
Glitter from worthless tins and broken glass.
His blue eyes are reflected from pools in the gutter,
And his strength is the desolate stone of fallen cities.

Oh in the kitchen-midden of my dreams
Turning over the potsherds of past days
Shall I uncover his loved desecrated face?
Are the unfathomed depths of sleep his grave?

Beyond the looming dangerous end of night
Beneath the vaults of fear do his bones lie,
And does the maze of nightmare lead to the power within?
Do menacing nether waters cover the fish king?

I piece the divine fragments into the mandala
Whose centre is the lost creative power,
The sun, the heart of God, the lotus, the electron
That pulses world upon world, ray upon ray
That he who lived on the first may rise on the last day.

THE HERM

Blind I know with senses rising from fern and tree,
Blind lips and fingers trace a god no eyes can see,
Blind I touch love's monster form that bounds
My world of field and forest, crowns my hills.
Blind I worship a blind god in his hour
Whose serpent-wand over my soul has power
To lead the crowning souls back from the borders of death,
Heaven's swift-winged fiat, earth's primeval monolith.

EUDAIMON

Bound and free,
I to you, you to me,
We parted at the gate
Of childhood's house, I bound,
You free to ebb and flow
In that life-giving sea
In whose dark womb
I drowned.

In a dark night
In flight unbounded
You bore me bound
To my prison-house,
Whose window invisible bars
From mine your world.

Your life my death
Weeps in the night
Your freedom bound
To me, though bound still free
To leave my tomb,

On wings invisible
To span the night and all the stars,
Pure liquid and serene,
I you, you me,
There one; on earth alone
I lie, you free.

ROSE

Gather while you may
Vapour of water, dust of earth, rose
Of air and water and light that comes and goes:
Over and over again the rose is woven.

Who knows the beginning?
In the vein in the sun in the rain
In the rock in the light in the night there is none.
What moves light over water? An impulse
Of rose like the delight of girl's breasts
When the nipples bud and grow a woman
Where there was a child, a woman to bear
A child unbegun (is there
Anywhere one? Are the people of dreams
Waiting — where? — to be born?) Does the green
Bud rose without end contain?
Within green sepals, green cells, you find none.
The crude
Moist, hard, green and cold
Petal on petal unfolding rose from nowhere.

But the perfect form is moving
Through time, the rose is a transit, a wave that weaves
Water, and petals fall like notes in order;
No more rose on ground unbecome
Unwoven unwound are dust are formless
And the rose is over but where
Labours for ever the weaver of roses?

STATUES

they more than we are what we are,
Serenity and joy
We lost or never found,
The forms of heart's desire,
We gave them what we could not keep,
We made them what we cannot be.

Their kingdom is our dream, but who can say
If they or we
Are dream ore dreamer, signet or clay;
If the most perfect be most true
These faces pure, these bodies poised in thought
Are substance of our form,
And we the confused shadows cast.

Growing towards their prime, they take our years away,
And from our deaths they rise
Immortal in the life we lose.
The gods consume us, but restore
More than we were:
We love, that they may be,
They are, that we may know.

HEIRLOOM

She gave me childhood's flowers,
Heather and wild thyme,
Eyebright and tormentil,
Lichen's mealy cup
Dry on wind-scored stone,
The corbies on the rock,
The rowan by the burn.

Sea-marvels a child beheld
Out in the fisherman's boat,
Fringed pulsing violet
Medusa, sea-gooseberries,
Starfish on the sea-floor,
Cowries and rainbow-shells
From pools on a rocky shore,

Gave me her memories,
But kept her last treasure:
'When I was a lass', she said,
'Sitting among the heather,
'Suddenly I saw
'That all the moor was alive!
'I have told no-one before'.

That was my mother's tale.
Seventy years had gone
Since she saw the living skein
Of which the world is woven,
And having seen, knew all;
Through long indifferent years
Treasuring the priceless pearl.

JUDAS-TREE

When first I heard that story it seemed incredible
That one betrayed;
But now, having lived my own, more wonderful
That eleven stayed
Even so precariously, so stupidly, so tentatively faithful.
So few are true; and I,
In others as in myself despising him who died,
Not once but many times have done what Judas did,
Yet sorrowed less than he,
For I still live, not hang on any purple blossoming tree.

4 Poems From
ON A DESERTED SHORE

13
We do not hear the harmony
That sounds about us everywhere;
Sense bleeds on iron and thorns
Of rock and fire
Until death breaks the elemental forms
To free the music of the spheres
That builds all worlds continually.

14
They pass into that music:
I too in sleep have heard
The harmony sublime
And known myself among the blessed dead.
We cannot walk the waves they tread,
For the earth of heaven is sound,
To sense this stony ground:
They hear as music what we feel as pain.

82
Original sin:
I stand condemned, being born,
To cast the human shadow;
We darken each our sun,
Who have not done, but are, that wrong.

100
Into your boundless state
All night afloat
On lift and fall of the great sea
Rocks in the bay my anchored boat.

SORROW, SORROW

Sorrow, sorrow
Inwoven with these skies, these seas,
Sun's smile and shadow
Over still hills moving mist and cloud,
Gull and gannet in flight, eider at rest on the wave,
Plunge and soaring of life, seabird's lonely cry,
Yellow iris where the seaweed dries
On shell strewn grass above the tide
And on the thorn the sweet white rose:
My heart no longer knows
an old sorrow from an older joy.

An Interview with Kathleen Raine

BRIAN KEEBLE

10 December 1977

Dr. Raine, how did you begin as a poet?

My mother wrote down my first poems before I could hold a pencil. I think the reason I became a poet was because I was born into a family to which poetry mattered very much. My father was an English master and taught literature at the local County High School and poetry was my mother's life. She knew great quantities of poetry by heart, by Milton in particular and the other English romantic poets. Also she was Scotch and knew by heart a great deal of the Scottish oral tradition, the poetry that had come down to her through that inheritance, so in my childhood I was in an environment of poetry. It was really through my mother that I became a poet; I think there's little doubt of that. And I continued to grow up in a household in which literature was held in high esteem. I had an excellent grounding in poetry and literature through my home, more than through my school. It was simply a household where there were books on the shelves, where my mother very naturally discussed poetry and recited it. It was the air I breathed.

How did you learn the actual craft of poetry? Was this through your parents or at a later stage?

It was really through my parents. I was at an excellent girls' County High School where we learnt that sort of thing. Schools were more conventional in those days and so we did learn the basic English meters. My father also taught me a good deal about metrics. It so happened that this interested him very much. He was more interested in the structure of language and metrics than perhaps he was in the more romantic side of poetry, which was my mother's concern. He did, in fact, teach me, and I remember it with great pleasure, the classical lyric meters. I didn't learn Latin in school, my father taught it to me. And he taught me a great deal about Latin metrics and the meters of Horace which, of course, are Greek meters. It was a very happy experience to learn these things from my father.

When you speak of your father teaching you, did he teach you as a practicing poet himself?

No, my father was a teacher. He could teach anyone anything. He loved literature, but it never occurred to him to practice it himself. He had a very clear and exact mind, and he was deeply interested in the structure and metrics of language. He not only knew Latin but Anglo-Saxon very well. I was too idle, I'm afraid, to learn Anglo-Saxon, but he taught me a little of the Anglo-Saxon metrics. These things were what he loved.

You have done some teaching yourself in the formal sense, both at Girton College and at Morley College. In what direction and to what works would you direct a young poet today seriously wanting to learn the craft of verse?

I think he should simply read the whole of English literature. There is no way of learning about literature except by reading literature. The first steps are always rather unproductive, but as you know more so you take more pleasure in seeing the relation, the development of ideas, the channels through which images flow, the changes that come over a literature in the course of time. In fact there is no other way, as Yeats says: "Nor is there singing school but studying monuments of its own magnificence". You simply must read the literature of your own language, and this I did. When I was educated, we were taught French up to quite a high standard, and I've also read a good deal of French literature with great pleasure, much less of Latin, and a very little Italian. I've simply followed Dante with a translation on the other side. But that is the only way to become a poet, to read poetry, to study poetry, and as you know more so you see more into the development of the language and the way in which it changes and where you yourself pick up the thread. All these things can't be taught. They can only be learned, they can only be discovered in the course of experiencing them for yourself. There are no short cuts. I'm afraid this is an age that wants a quick solution to every problem and to have some small formula which gives you instant knowledge. But knowledge cannot be had at the cheap rate that this age demands, in any sphere, including that of literature and the arts. The long slow hard way is the only way to achieve excellence in any field. And literature is no exception.

May I suggest that perhaps one might have thought that a poet of your cast of mind would have made more use of traditional forms, whereas in fact very few of your poems are in traditional stanzaic strict forms. Does this reflect or indicate anything about your attitude towards those forms? It's particularly interesting in view of the fact you told me earlier about your father teaching you a great deal about metrics.

When you come to write a poem it's a very different thing from doing an exercise in metrics, because when you are analyzing the metrics of older poets you have the poem before you and you dissect what is there. When you are writing a poem the pre-existing form does not exist. The form is what comes at the end of the process of writing the poem, not at the beginning. Therefore you are approaching it from the other end. I believe the pre-existing forms that we know were spontaneous and came as the natural forms in which certain ideas embodied themselves at certain times for certain poets. The sonnet form, for example, seemed to come so naturally to Renaissance poets, both Italian and English. Now, I know how a sonnet is put together; I could answer an examination paper probably, more or less, on the different forms of sonnets perfectly well. But if I myself were to write a sonnet this would be a fabrication; a poem would not naturally come to me in sonnet form. The form in which a poem comes is a living form. You have to accept the form that comes to you. Perhaps the sonnet has been written too often. It represents a certain shape of an idea, very beautiful when it comes in that form. Shakespeare's sonnets, you know, are so unified and so beautiful. I must say that by the time one gets to Wordsworth the sonnet is already a little tedious, I find. Hopkins perhaps brought it to life again.

Of course I could write a sonnet; I could write any of these forms, but it wouldn't be an imaginative act. It would be a fabrication, an imitation, something which would come from my rational mind and not from my imagination. Forms are born from the imagination, but they are constructed by the reason. My forms come to me as they must, born from the imagination. I don't construct them by reason; I'm not a poet of that kind. I feel I'm almost apologizing for the narrow range of my poems, but in a sense there are certain forms which I use in poetry. There are certain kinds of rhythmic patterns which I can recognize in my poems as being right. I don't use full rhyme very much, but I do attend very much to the rhyme structure of my poems. The recurring or half rhyme in what I write, both at the end of line and also within lines, is very carefully structured if you look at it. Someone else might be able to work it out as a pattern. I couldn't myself because I do it by instinct; but I do it very carefully and I know when it's right. Just lately I have been writing poems of three or four or five lines which are not constructed according to the Japanese Haiku pattern but are rather akin to the Haiku, in which every syllable is related to every other syllable. They look easy, but they're not. They are very structured forms, in reality, very small structured forms like diatoms or minute organic forms. But, again, in the last few years I have felt a compulsion to write in this particular form. They are, as it were, given me. This is what I mean when I say that what we call sapphics and alchaics and sonnets and villanelles and all these things probably were the forms that presented themselves to the imagination of certain poets at certain times. I don't believe they set out to write them in quite that way. They were the shape imagination was taking at certain periods.

The imagination presents its own forms in a very scrupulous manner. One can be very dishonest in falling into an easy form which rhymes and has a strict meter. One can be carried along with it, one can be carried away with it. Of course I know that Yeats used the splendid structured verse he did, traditional meters if you like, but he recreated them for his own purposes and they bear his individual stamp. I think

every poet, every true poet, leaves his own individual signature on the verse forms of the language that he uses. Edgar Allen Poe or Shelley or whoever it may be. I may have left a small signature in some of my forms; I think that it would be possible for some young literary critic fifty years from now to say, yes, this is a poem by Kathleen. And that is because and in so far as it comes from the imagination. Of course, I'm not foolish enough to think that women are ever going to produce the greatest art in any field. Women will always be, as it were, minor artists. And I think I see myself as a minor poet to whom certain minor forms have presented themselves. You know, the thought of writing a poem on the scale of a Milton or a Dante—one couldn't envisage it. And so the forms that come from my particular imagination are such as you find in my work. I think when I was younger I was sometimes carried away and added clever allusions, rather defensively. But now I feel confident of my verse forms; I know how to do it. This comes only with practice.

You made a mention earlier of pre-existing forms. One thinks immediately of Shelley, how he somehow had a sense of the form before he actually found something to put into the form. Do you think it's more a question of the poet attuning his imagination to this pre-existing form rather than a question of going through the mechanics?

Yes, of course it is. Shelley was like a great musician; his verse came to him in great inspired cadences of speech, before he had the words to put in it. You can see in his notebooks how these great cadences of verse presented themselves to his imagination, and he couldn't find the words rapidly enough to fill them. I found this myself in writing poems, that very often what presents itself is a cadence. One can't always find the words that go to the cadence immediately; that takes a little time. But the cadence comes.

Do you find yourself becoming a sort of rhythmic vessel, as it were?

A rhythmic vessel. Yes, like that. That's how they come.

Speaking now as a mature poet, when you're actually working on a poem have you encountered any impoverishment in current language?

I do find certain difficulties. There are words which, when I was young, I would have used without hesitation because they were current in educated speech. Sometimes I do pause and think, ah, that word may well be obsolete. I do in my writing use a very simple vocabulary, which is probably deceptive because in fact the ideas which are often implicit are not simple. But I do very much try to use simple words. Cleverness, you see, is wasted nowadays. When I was young, contemporaries of mine like William Empson, who was a Wykehamist and a scholar at Magdalene College and so on, could air his undergraduate cleverness, and we all enjoyed that very much because that kind of display of erudition was acceptable within that social group. The ideas were in fact not at all profound. It was simply the style that was erudite and enjoyable in a certain social context. I can't do that, and it seems rather childish to wish to do so, because, of course, profound ideas can be communicated in very simple words as we can see from, well, the Gospels for example. It is a matter of the resonance and depth that one can put into a simple language, not the size of one's vocabulary that counts.

Of course one isn't always sure that people are going to pick up the resonances of one's work, even though the words taken word by word are simple and understandable to anyone. I think this is the central problem in a way. I can't tell what the reader is going to bring to my poems, but as I work on the poem I try to translate into simple words ideas which perhaps come from a great deal of knowledge of various kinds in many books which the reader is not going to have read. And how is one going to be sure that the resonance will evoke anything in the reader? There one must simply rely on the fact that in any generation and at any time a human being is still possessed of the levels to which poetry speaks. In a materialist age people still have souls even if they may deny it. One addresses oneself in the poem to the level at which one hopes to be understood, hoping that although a given reader may not have read the same books as oneself or attained knowledge through the same channels, yet there will be an awareness that receives that which is communicated in the poem. That is the whole art of writing a poem, to make this kind of choice, to try to use valid signs, as David Jones would say; and the question of what are valid signs is a great problem. I think my poems are more accessible than say David Jones's because I use nature and cosmology rather than history, because the cosmos is new everyday. We awake within the creation. Every morning the sun rises; the world is created, and created at all its levels. If one relied on history, then I think the signs of history that used to be valid are probably no longer valid now. I think David Jones and T. S. Eliot were at a watershed in this respect. On the far side of that watershed we cannot rely on the historic symbols in the same way as Eliot could or David Jones. We have to use perhaps cosmological symbols which are unaging, rather than symbols from human history. After all, a great deal of the poetry of the Psalms, the poetry of the Old Testament, is entirely written in terms of the elements of nature, which one can find today just as much as one could then. This is, I suppose, my defense of my own attempt to use nature in my poetry, which is in any case a natural bent of my own, because these are the things I love.

You mentioned in the Preface to your Collected Poems *that you in fact dropped the poems that made use of ecclesiastical symbols, and it is evident in your poetry that you make use of the more immediate symbols of light and water and air. Do you find these are more evocative, more direct in relation to the problem of shared backgrounds?*

Yes. After all, the ecclesiastical symbols, as you call them, which every cultural tradition possesses—certain things used in a special way—in turn are all finally rooted in water, air, light, the growth of a plant, animation, different animal symbols. It all comes back to the immediate language which God speaks to every man every day, in the rising of the sun, the darkness and light, growth, the flowing of water, the crossing of the sea. All these things are the foundations of all symbolic traditions, finally. They take on more specialized meanings at certain cultural periods, certainly. And when I use, for example, wind or light or reflection in my poetry, I am perfectly aware of at least the Neoplatonic or Christian uses of these symbols, but they have to be restated in such a way that the reader can discover them anew. So I am

aware of how such a symbol comes to us loaded with the experience of generations of human beings who have experienced these things immediately from nature and who have also experienced them in some metaphysical tradition, but one has to cleanse them and try to represent them without losing any of the meaning which say Plotinus, or whoever it may be, has given to these symbols, and do so without actually mentioning or invoking Plotinus. If you have to put in the name of Plotinus, you are really confessing defeat as a poet, because the poem should communicate without that.

I feel this is a quality you share with, for instance, Vernon Watkins in his use of the symbol of light. It's perfectly possible to read through a poem by Watkins and appreciate the symbol of light which is underneath most of his poetry, and yet at another level one can associate it with Neoplatonic doctrine. I was very interested to read recently in a book on Watkins that he actually kept the Enneads *on his desk. Did you know that?*

Yes, I remember him telling me so. That's something we have in common because I keep the *Enneads* near also. Watkins is an excellent example of what I mean, because, as you say, it is possible to read him without knowing the *Enneads*, and yet we would agree that he does in his poems embody all that he needs from the *Enneads* without having to underline the fact that he is drawing on this source.

It seems as if he is speaking of the natural world, but there is no doubt that it is a natural world transfigured, not just a material world of corporeal light, as Blake may have said.

Indeed it is. But, you see, according to the depth of our understanding, so the world we perceive reflects that depth. As Blake said, ''A fool does not see the same tree that a wise man sees''. Vernon Watkins was really experiencing the physical world in a totally different way from the materialist, I suppose, because the light he saw was filled with a spiritual illumination as well as a physical visibility. He was giving in his poems a living experience, his own living experience of real light as he saw it from his little house on the west coast of the Gower Peninsula. When he saw the light on the sea, he experienced that light in terms of the depth of his own knowledge, so there is a meeting of the knowledge and the actual corporeal experience which comes through in the poetry. It isn't that everyone sees the world in exactly the same way, but some people add a little metaphysics from a tradition and others don't do so. The experience itself of seeing is transformed, as we transform ourselves by the depth of our own understanding of the world, which comes to us through many channels—through life and through learning and through reading the great books of all religions.

The question of the poet having his metaphysics in his heart rather than in his head.

Oh, certainly. It is only the metaphysics that the poet has in his heart that is the slightest use in his poetry. If poets have their metaphysics in their heads only and try to write verse, it doesn't work. It is only living experience that emerges in poetry, and this is just as true of the experience of the intellect as it is of the physical experience. Dante lived his metaphysics. It wasn't something he knew and added to his earthly experience; it was experience of the heart. That is why poetry and the arts are so testing, because you can't get away with falsehood. The poem will only tell the truth that you know with your whole life and being. Anything added is just trimmings. It's nothing at all. You can bespat-

ter your verses with all kinds of learned allusions, but it doesn't in the least communicate the knowledge that the names you may put in are intended to communicate. You can only communicate what you have lived in a work of art.

Do you think that Eliot and Pound were to some degree guilty of this?

I think Eliot and Pound are very different. Pound was a man of letters. He really became excited by literature; it had a magical spell for him, and he managed to communicate this. His love for a certain range of literature communicates itself in his work. I was thinking of poets not nearly so good as Pound, although Pound isn't my favorite poet. But I would give him his due, that his enthusiasm for letters was probably the most authentic thing about him. I think Eliot used those learned allusions of his in a different way. I feel they were rather the mask, or the comouflage almost, with which a very passionate and tormented soul gave a kind of dignity to passions that were perhaps so searing and so intimately personal that he couldn't have endured to expose them more nakedly. He was using a seemly mask by invoking Lancelot Andrewes and that rather dignified procession of names that we find in his work. When I read *The Waste Land* now I am struck not so much by the learned allusions that need footnotes, which indeed did impress us when we were young, but by the anguish behind that mask of dignity which he had to assume for his own protection.

One gets the impression from so much poetry today that poets are desperately trying to manipulate the limbs of an organism that is essentially dead, or at least it will not yield quite what they want it to, and that leads to some desperate innovations, at its worst, for example, concrete poetry.

I think it yields exactly what they want it to. I think it's a great fallacy that poetry is somehow going to save the culture to which it belongs. In fact, poetry can only express the culture from which it springs, and this kind of rubbish that one sees so much of, which is as you say totally bankrupt, is expressing only too well the bankrupt situation of materialist society. The materialist view of reality is in its very nature incapable of producing great art, because it denies those levels of the human being from which imagination speaks and of which poetry and music and the other arts are the language. If you deny the soul and the spirit you have cut off the possibility of the very expression of the soul and the spirit, which is art. You cannot have poetry which comes only from the material level of experience. It is simply not possible. Naturally poetry is bankrupt. You can have on that level, if you like, political verse, you can have wit, you can have to a certain extent, although one sees all too little of it, comic verse. You could even have, in a more elegant age, the mannered verse of the Augustan poets. But if you deny the reality of the human soul and the spirit which informs it, poetry ceases to be possible, because poetry at its greatest, as I understand it, is the language of the human soul, through which the spirit speaks. It is not the language of the temporal human being in a material world. And if these people were honest, they would say they have no use for poetry and the other arts in their kind of world, but they're not honest. I suppose they think they can still derive some sort of prestige from the name of poet which came from other ages in which poetry had a real meaning and function in society. But "poet" has almost become a word one can't use nowadays. One is ashamed to say one is a poet when one considers what we've come to. The kinds of things you are referring to like concrete poetry are just rubbish, of course, more or less harmless. Hamilton Finlay's

garden is a rather pleasant, imaginative spot, but it's of no importance in point of view of poetry. It is in a sense rather magical; I think that he's a sort of poor man's Capability Brown, and I've no wish to decry this. But we poets are trying to do something different.

Can you say something about the difference between what you refer to, in speaking of your own work, as a simple style in contrast to a colloquial idiom?

By the colloquial idiom I think you mean the kind of poetry that accepts with the colloquialisms the whole world that they imply. The poet is putting himself on the level of the colloquialisms, rather than raising the level of discourse, as Blake, for example, did in *Songs of Innocence* by giving people simple words upon which they can ascend to the meaning of the poet. The poet comes down to the level of his readers rather than leading the readers, through words that are familiar to them, up to the level of the poet. I think that many poets do like to come down to the level of the readers, presumably in order to have readers. I don't know whether it works; it probably doesn't, in the long run.

On what grounds must the battle for the future of poetry be fought if it is to survive being buried beneath the accumulated detritus of what we are pleased to call culture these days?

It can't be buried, because humanity doesn't change. Reality is always what it is, and human beings are not in reality different now than in any other age. Fashion can't change the real nature of man; and because man is man and we have in ourselves a certain nature which responds to certain themes and experiences, I believe it is always possible for a great poet who speaks from the fullness of his humanity to find a response in other human beings who share that humanity. The function of the arts is surely to awaken in people self-knowledge, knowledge of the scope and scale of their own humanity which they may not have been aware of. It is an enlargement of experience. In almost every respect Yeats's view of the kind of world we live in is diametrically opposite to the kind of world which is put about by the mass media. Yet what a response Yeats has awakened by his poetry in many people who couldn't have accepted the ground from which it undoubtedly grew. Now we see that people are even beginning to take his ideas seriously because they have come to realize through his poetry some of the depth from which that poetry itself arose. I think it can always be done. The question is the genius of the poet. If one is good enough one can awaken the response in human beings that one would wish to awake. In fact one awakens by one's work exactly that level in other people to which the work is adequate. Of course there are a great many people who don't respond, but some do. I would never despair. I don't think that the mere fact that we are in a very low and dark period culturally is any excuse for poets not writing to the height of their powers; in fact you have to be rather better than not so good. You have to aim even higher in order to get your response, not lower, in such an age. It's a great mistake to think that by coming down and writing colloquial idiom you will do this. You won't. You will do it perhaps by being as good as Yeats.

Much of your poet's learning has taken place at the confluence of the traditions of both East and West. How do you view the apparent abandonment of all that was meant by a classical education in favor of what appears to be, in the hands of the young, a cursory knowledge of the traditions of the East?

Well, of course I greatly regret the abandonment of such treasures of civilization as we have in the West, without in the least wishing to discourage anyone from searching in the East or in any other tradition. It is not what the young are learning from the East that I deplore, but what they are not learning from the West. In fact knowledge is always good and ignorance is always bad. The crossroad situation is one in which I have certainly felt myself very much involved; I have read a certain amount of Eastern philosophy, from which I have received a great deal of enlightenment of my own tradition. In fact, Christianity seems plausible in the light of Indian Buddhist and Vedantic teaching in a way that it never seemed plausible to me as it was presented by the rather unenlightened teachers from whom I received it as a child. I think that every tradition can receive replenishment from other traditions without one's having to abandon one's own. This seems to me to be a good thing. Of course I do regret the failure of our own tradition; that is very regrettable. But I don't regret the curiosity about other traditions, and I find the hippies and the generation who have been making their pilgrimages to the Far East very touching. They may learn at a very superficial level, but at least they are seeking for something. I don't deplore their search. I may deplore their ignorance, but not their search.

I think it was Coomaraswamy who made the point that the only real reason to have a knowledge of another tradition is that that knowledge should plunge one back into the roots of one's own tradition.

Yes, I think this is very important because any religious tradition, at least Vedanta certainly, and the American Indian too, would say that the time and place into which we are born is no accident. We are born exactly where it is appropriate for us to be, and therefore we must not deny that which we receive by being born where we are. We can't remake ourselves. I have tried very hard, as you know, for a whole lifetime to make a Christian of myself, simply on those grounds. I felt I was born within what one may call Christendom and must make the best of a bad job, if you like. I have often felt that I very much wished I were born elsewhere and in another time. I would much rather, so I have fancied, to have been born in the time and place of Pythagoras or Plotinus, or maybe in India or in Buddhist Japan, but as this has not been the case I felt it was necessary to come to terms with who one is and where one has been situated. I think David Jones also felt this was very important. We must use what comes to our hands. Of course, what comes to the hand of anyone born in the modern world, the second half of the twentieth century, is a situation of the confluence of cultures, and it would be just as artificial to exclude other cultures as it would be to abandon one's own. One cannot any longer be the kind of Christian that was possible in the seventeenth century, for example, who was totally ignorant of other religions. It is very noticeable among my various friends who are interested in the perennial philosophy in one way or another that they all speak of the necessity of adopting one tradition, but many of them have not adopted the tradition to which they were born. I think this is a situation of mixing cultures which we can't exclude at this time. One can't exclude what comes to one, because there it is; it comes. It's rather difficult to keep one's bearings in this situation, and very important to do so—also very exciting to do so. I find it a very enriching and living experience to live at this time.

Of course knowledge of the classical world has again and again proved itself capable of being a regenerative experience, hasn't it?

I think our Western European tradition, by which I mean the Platonic and Neoplatonic metaphysics, has been equal to any other tradition. There is no need to go further afield; it is all there and very splendid and full. It lacks nothing of the completeness of any other tradition of the perennial philosophy. When I was young, knowledge of the Greek myths was almost taken for granted; one learned them as a child. There were countless books for children or for young people about Greek mythology; this was in every child's ordinary upbringing. I certainly learnt all these things long before I went to school. I found in teaching at Girton College, Cambridge, that the students did not know the classical myths, and I think it is a great loss to the younger generation now. But certainly wherever the Neoplatonic tradition has surfaced in Western culture, as at the time of the Renaissance or of the Romantic Poets in England or in Germany or again in the Irish Renaissance, it has always had a power of fertilizing and regenerating the poetry or the thought of its time. Truth never becomes out of date; it is always itself and is always there for those who wish to avail themselves of it. It can never lose its validity.

If I may come back to your own work for a moment, it could be said that in its entirety your work throws out a challenge to the values of the contemporary literary world.

Certainly my work throws out, if you like, a challenge, but I don't think of it as a challenge to the received values of the world I live in, but rather as an attempt to affirm the enduring values insofar as I have discovered them. This I have tried to do in various ways, as you know: in my Blake scholarship, in such criticisms as I have written, in my work on Thomas Taylor, and in my poetry certainly. This is the ground from which my poetry comes. I'm not concerned with the literary world. There you've touched on a very important point as far as I'm concerned. I don't see the literary world as something in itself. There is no such thing. The literary world, as I said earlier, poetry, is only expressing the culture in which it is rooted. Insofar as what you call the literary world is an expression of current ideologies, that doesn't concern me at all. It is a different order of values from my own work. I am trying to embody certain realizations which over the course of a lifetime I have come to value. In a way, you see, I am speaking to the people who belong to a different culture from what you call the literary world, which is only the articulation of the culture for which it speaks. I have nothing in common with another person just because he happens to write verse. The people with whom I have something in common are the ones who share my premises and experience of reality. There used to be talk about two cultures, and I very much believe there are two cultures, but the division doesn't come between the literary world and the non-literary world; it comes in a different direction altogether. It comes in a certain view of man. There is the culture of a materialist view of man, which, as I take it, underlies the kind of colloquial verse you were speaking of earlier, and there is the culture of the spiritual view of man. And that for me is where the division comes. I have everything in common with those,

whether of the past or of the present, who participate in the spiritual view of man and nothing in common with the others. I know myself to be to a great extent, though not totally, isolated as I stand now. After all, I have on my side the great poets of the past and many of my contemporaries, for example my contemporaries whom I have known among my friends: David Gascoyne, Edwin Muir, T. S. Eliot. I didn't actually know Yeats though I did know Mrs. Yeats after his death. One doesn't feel all that isolated, you know, because the spiritual view of man has never been totally destroyed in the world.

When I was young, you see, literacy was rather different. One had something in common with people because there was a certain level of what one might call secular culture, which was a shared common ground between believers and non-believers over a certain area. And there is a certain spiritual resonance, for example, in, well Proust obviously. Who could say whether Proust was a believer or non-believer; it hardly matters. He had a certain imaginative depth and resonance, as did even Virginia Woolf in certain areas of her experience—there was an overlap. Now I feel that with secular culture, the division is really much more clear-cut. There is really literally nothing in common between the profane culture of this time and the other side which I try to express. I think the rift is much clearer. It's perhaps regrettable that there no longer is any common ground of the old European secular culture on a very high level, which existed up to the middle of the Second World War but seems to have disappeared since. I literally find I have nothing in common with secular, or rather indeed one can only say profane, writers who have no spiritual root in their work. That I think is a very painful thing, to be in such a situation. It was much happier in the old days when there was this area of common ground, where one could share certain values which belonged to European civilization, which of course originally had its spiritual roots. And a great deal of this still continued in modes of feeling, manners if you like, modes of behavior, which though not immediately rooted in a spiritual vision were ultimately rooted in a civilization which had itself had roots. In fact European Christendom has now virtually ceased to exist in this country. I think it still lingers on in France, where I feel very much more at home than I do in England, culturally speaking, or maybe in Spain. I may be over-optimistic in that, because I think the whole thing is doomed.

You have often observed that in our time ignorance sits in judgment over knowledge. Could you spell out some of the more dangerous varieties of this disease?

I think the most dangerous variety of the disease is to suppose that man exists only on a horizontal plane, as a biological being in a material world. It is the discounting of what one might call the vertical dimensions of our humanity that is most dangerous. You see, materialism tries to reduce all things to the quantifiable. Now life cannot be quantified, consciousness cannot be quantified; and by saying that only the quantifiable is real, by identifying reality with the materially measurable and materially quantifiable, you are in fact cutting away the greater part of our humanity, which is not quantifiable, which exists in, one can but say, higher dimensions. Life, consciousness, self-consciousness: these are all degrees and modes of experience which cannot be evaluated in material terms. And insofar as materialist philosophy tries to reduce consciousness, for example, to the organ of the brain through which consciousness is registered, it is trying always to reduce the higher experience to some lower terms than itself, instead of seeing the

lower, quantifiable, material level as itself a reflection which is created by the higher levels of reality. In fact, I think the most dangerous of all illusions is to suppose that the material world completely accounts for all reality and all human experience. Far the most dangerous.

As an autonomous world, in fact.

As an autonomous world, yes. That is *the* heresy.

As a writer who has borne witness to a very different set of values to those commonly operative in our society, what has it meant to you to be constantly going against the grain in this way?

Well, I've found it very invigorating insofar as my scholarship is concerned. It's given me something that I felt was important to do. It has seemed to me worthwhile doing this even though I may not be the most qualified person to do it; at least it meant that what I was doing had a real value. It has been a challenge, and I've very much enjoyed it. I am very happy to have had the opportunity of doing this particular piece of work in my time and place.

Now that the culture wallahs, as David Jones might call them, have capitulated so completely to the entertainment wallahs, would you go so far as to say that we are living in times that are without culture?

Pretty nearly so.

One often meets with the expressed fear of the breakdown of culture. At what point does culture break down for you?

I think when the allusions are no longer received. You see, in any work of art the subtle allusions that one is constantly making, not necessarily quotations from Shakespeare, but words and ideas, are used on the supposition that the reader is going to share that ground sufficiently to respond to certain symbols. If one said the Cup are they going to think of the Grail, or if one said the Cave are they going to think of Plato? These are rather poor examples, but all the time the poet is working upon a shared background of language and literature and religion and history, which one has to play on like an instrument. One sounds the language like a sounding board on the supposition that within one's own society people will know what one is talking about and respond to those allusions which are the essence of communication. When this is no longer so, then that culture has broken down. I think we've come very near that point now.

In your recent paper on David Jones you mentioned the scholar Edith Hamilton's definition of a barbarian as someone who does not know his or her past.

Yes, who has no past. And against that one could place T. S. Eliot's remark, I hope I quote it correctly: "We know more than the past; yes, and the past is what we know". Within a civilization the whole of the past is contemporaneous. We read Homer, and Achilles and that great battle outside Troy becomes for us contemporaneous; it is part of our present. The life of Jesus Christ is contemporaneous. This is the quality of the mind: all things within the regions of the mind exist contemporaneously. All are just as present to us as what we hear on the news this evening. It is a terrible situation when the present of people is so narrow that it only includes what happened to them this week. This is terrible. The whole purpose of human culture and civilization is to expand the area of the present to include great areas of the past, remote other times, other lives, other civilizations. A truly civilized person is one whose interior experience embraces great areas of what has happened in the past and in other cultures. To be an uncultured person is to have none of this.

A cultured person would indeed be able to relate the historical process itself, however broadly, to that which was above and beyond the historical process as well, do you think?

Well, I was speaking then only of culture, and I would say that culture has broken down when a total body of knowledge which belongs to a civilization is no longer a shared knowledge. But, of course, beyond that every great civilization has in fact itself been rooted in some metaphysical vision or premise, from which its culture has flowered, as Christendom flowered from the vision which came into being at the time of Christ. And all its art, its music, its expression has, as it were, been like the foliage born on that tree. And so with Islam or with Far Eastern Buddhist civilization; it always is the flower. Of course, the culture is the flower on some living root of that kind, and that is certainly very important.

Would you say that for the poet culture is inherent in the accumulated connotations of words?

Yes, and that was why earlier, when you asked me what the best training for a poet was, I said to read the whole of the literature of that language, because that is the way in which we become familiar with the meanings of words, their connotations, their resonances, which is the instrument upon which any poem must play. And when these illusions, connotations, resonances are lost to a society as a whole, then poetry of real quality becomes impossible, quite apart from the metaphysics of the situation. This is purely on a cultural level. There, I would say, is the breaking-down point of culture which you asked me just now—when the words no longer are embedded in the total matrix of a language which itself is the total product of a culture reaching back to the very beginnings of language. It is only from the whole of a culture that words derive any meaning whatsoever. There is nothing inherently meaningful in a word. A word is simply a magical sign that in the course of history has gathered about itself certain meanings. Therefore, the only way in which a poet can use words with mastery is to familiarize himself with words in the context in which they have been used. The same applies to verse forms; you will learn better how to use verse forms by familiarizing yourself with the works of those poets who have used those forms than by taking an abstract pattern and trying to use it yourself. You can't isolate one part of a language. Self-expression is really a fallacious notion which is much too prevalent, because if we were really, totally left to our own resources and were expressing only ourselves we would have neither the words to expres ourselves with nor a context of culture which would make these words communicable to others.

I believe you destroyed your first attempt to write about Blake.

Yes, I did in fact do so. I didn't at the time possess the adequate knowledge for a study of Blake. I had seen, as many others have before and since, that the basic psychological pattern which Blake was uncovering was very similar to that described by Jung—you know, the fourfold structure of the psyche and the anima and so on— and my first attempt on Blake was rather a Jungian interpretation. However, at that time, Philip Sherrard lent me several books by René Guénon which completely transformed my view of the whole matter. The idea of a tradition of esoteric knowledge and an accompanying language of symbols was new to me, and I immediately, or very soon, realized that this was the key to Blake, that he was in fact working within a traditional language, using that traditional symbolic language in a strictly objective way, and was not to be understood in terms of a personal system, as many had previously thought, invented by himself. And this indeed proved to be the right key. After that I decided to discover where Blake had made his links with tradition and set myself the task of reading everything that he mentioned having read. By the time I had done so I had come upon a whole body of what one can only call excluded knowledge upon which he was drawing: knowledge in fact of the spiritual tradition which was based on premises other than the materialist society in which we are and indeed in which Blake was living. It is a very venerable tradition indeed, going back to Plato and the Neoplatonists. He knew a little of the Vedanta, he knew something of Cabbala; fewer texts were available to Blake than are available to us, but at least he drew upon a coherent tradition of knowledge based on the premise that mind or spirit is the ground of reality and not matter. And that was the key.

Was it your work on Blake or your reading of Jung that was instrumental in desolidifying what must have seemed the exclusively positivist and materialist world of your Cambridge days?

It was both. In so far as Jung was more immediately accessible, I suppose he came first, because, as I've just said, I was reading Jung before I was reading tradition. Certainly he achieved a great deal of desolidification, but I had no conception of the strength of the traditional position until I had done a very great deal of reading in relation to my work on Blake. And it was like melting an iceberg, but the iceberg really totally disappeared by the time I'd covered all the ground of this beautiful, coherent, and highly reasonable body of philosophy and knowledge.

Your frequent references to Jungian ideas have about them a certain note of ambivalence. You speak of him as being the one teacher of your generation to whom you are most indebted, yet you also claim you are not a Jungian. Can you explain?

I would never commit myself totally to being a follower of anyone, not even William Blake. In fact, Jung and Blake derived their particular knowledge both from the same sources. Both were deeply versed in Gnostic literature, for example. Jung, I think, had a particular function to perform, which was to reopen in this century the inner worlds which had been virtually lost. Certainly Freud discovered, or rediscovered, the unconscious, but he did not for a moment realize what a great continent he had in fact discovered. I think it was Jung who realized this, that the inner worlds are not simply regions of knowledge repressed from consciousness. Freud's philosophy is really a materialist philosophy: there is nothing in the unconscious that hasn't come through the world of the senses. Jung realized that this is an area of life, that the psyche is living and has its own laws and its own structures and is to each individual an oracle in the heart which mediates from—he would never quite say, but he never quite unsays it either—a divine source to the human. I think Jung was very careful to keep his teaching within the terms of medical science, because he knew that if he did not do so he would be dismissed as a crank. From *Memories, Dreams, Reflections* we know that he did wholly believe in God and that the oracle in the heart he did see as the immediate presence of God to every individual. Now, I couldn't call myself a Jungian because I spent twenty-five years on showing that this was Blake's teaching. If I were to call myself an adherent of anyone, it would be Blake rather than Jung, because I think Blake put this more fully, more perfectly, more convincingly than even Jung did. But it is, of course, the same realization of the God within. The other reason why I could not totally call myself a Jungian is that tradition is not a purely subjective thing, that we cannot live entirely from inner revelation without the support, I think, of revealed tradition as this is understood by all the great religions. Such figures as the Buddha or Jesus Christ or Muhammad have a function within a total society to bring a new revelation to a whole group of people. Although we cannot experience these things otherwise than within the psyche, nevertheless a revealed tradition holds before us knowledge which we have to work towards, so I think the collective revelation is also important. We can't live entirely without that side, not entirely from the psyche.

You have written that Jung is less poetic than Plotinus or Proclus. Can you explain?

I can't remember when I said that or what I meant at the time, but what I perhaps meant was that the total cosmology of

Plotinus or the Neoplatonists is wider in its embrace than the psychology of Jung. The total cosmology of Platonism presumes four worlds, of which the psyche is one. Jung, without denying the existence of the other worlds, is speaking only of the psyche. Where he is of great importance is that it is within the psyche that we as human beings must experience the symbols which Plotinus, as a great mystic, also perhaps experienced on higher levels, levels which Jung leaves, with I think considerable tact, and perhaps because he himself was not concerned with them. But in defense of Jung I must say this, that it is within the psyche that we encounter reality; this is where the symbols come to meet us. We know that a certain symbol is valid when we encounter it in our own dreams or visions. There is no argument, because that is a living experience. From that point of view I think our debt to Jung in this age is boundless, because there's no question that the symbols of the churches and so on have become purely external and dead, unable to re-awaken in believers in a certain religion the living experience from which they originally sprang and which they, in an age of living faith, can mediate. Jung restored the living source. Of course, he didn't, as Plotinus did, relate this to a total cosmology; that wasn't in fact his function. He didn't deny a total cosmology, which I think Freud did. He is an open-ended psychologist; this is his great merit. Others like to close their systems, but Jung left his open.

Do you agree that some of the followers of Jung are in danger of blindly seeing the psyche as all?

Some may be and others not. There are a great many followers of Jung who are following their own religious tradition, as indeed Jung very much advised people to do. When he had, as it were, completed a cure, he very often found that the patient would spontaneously return to whatever religious tradition he had originally come from, and Jung regarded that as a very desirable end to achieve. There is nothing in Jungian psychology that is incompatible with the adherence to some religious tradition; on the contrary. On the other hand, no doubt there are Jungian psychologists who do not belong to such a tradition. And whether it would be possible to be a Jungian and an atheist, that I very much doubt. Jung himself said on the British television, when he was asked whether he believed in God, "That is a very difficult question because I don't believe, I know". Knowledge is different from belief, you see. Jung at least made that clear, I think, to all who have come under his influence, that to know a thing is a very vital experience, whereas believing can mean nothing at all.

You have mentioned that Marco Pallis considered the Neoplatonic learning as being dead. Yet there is, isn't there, something about that learning that poets refuse to let die? After all, Blake and Shelley and Yeats and Vernon Watkins and yourself have all found something living in this body of knowledge.

Yes. This is a very interesting point really, because Marco would not regard

Neoplatonism as a valid living tradition in which one could participate as one can participate in those religions which have, for example, a liturgy. Neoplatonism exists now only, if you like, in books. But as a poet it has for me been the most living tradition of all. I would never deny my Neoplatonism; I am a very knife-edge Christian indeed. The poets certainly have kept the tradition of Neoplatonism alive in Europe, whether within Christendom or outside it; it is the real religion of the poets. I think what Marco perhaps felt was lacking in Neoplatonism is something that Christian worship offers, which is a point of meeting between the wise and the ignorant, common humanity and learning: a point at which you can share the symbols at every level with people of every kind. I think this is most important, and it's something that I've felt as a lack, certainly, in my life. This is why I keep trying to go back to the Church, although I'm never very happy when I get there. But it is something that is very important to poets, not to live in an abstract world where there is no common language or shared symbolism with living people.

What do you understand by tradition?

You're leading me into very deep waters, Brian. Tradition is knowledge absolute of the nature of man and his place in the cosmos. Absolute, that is, in relation to our own human potentiality, because one cannot know beyond our humanity. Now this knowledge has been revealed in the several great religions of the world and indeed to primitive people within their own terms, even in the most simple cultures as, for example, the American Indians, whom I was fortunate to meet a year ago. It is sometimes called the perennial philosophy. It is true in an absolute sense no less so now than in the past or in the future.

Can you say what you don't mean by tradition?

Certainly I do not mean what Dr. Leavis meant by tradition, which was simply anything that may be handed on within a society from one writer to another, say style or subject matter, which could be true or untrue or valuable or less valuable; it would be simply the transmission of anything or everything from generation to generation. And this could include falsehood as well as truth; it could include the tradition that runs from Bacon to Newton and Locke to Darwin and so on. But this is not what is meant by tradition among those who have familiarized us with the kind of thought I am speaking of. People like Guenon, Coomaraswamy, and Marco Pallis use tradition, I think, in the sense of metaphysical knowledge revealed in an historical situation, of which every civilization has its own branch and form and prophet.

I know I speak for many people, including myself, who find that the many occasional essays you've written in recent years have acted as a sort of bridge of access from the somewhat confined world of English literature, contemporary literature, to the bigger world of tradition, its symbols, its doctrines and myths, etc. Do you regard this work of equal importance to your poetry?

No, in fact I don't. But it was work I had to do, not only as a piece of self-education, as it was when I began my studies on Blake, a sort of laying of the foundations, but for the reason you said, that one must provide a bridge of access of some kind. But, again, poetry is a living experience. These essays and works of scholarship, which have occupied a great deal of my time and have involved great labor, have in fact been works on the level of the rational mind, putting together the works of others, which is certainly relevant to the imaginative experience of poetry that I have tried to communicate. But, you see, that isn't a living speech. That is a construction which one perhaps has to make and has its value, but poetry is the thing itself. Poetry is the living language of living experience; poetry speaks from the soul, and that must always be a higher level than the other. But I must say that without laying these laborious foundations I don't think I could have written the poetry. This, I think, would have also been true of Yeats, who laid such laborious and firm foundations to his work, or indeed of William Blake, whom I found to my surprise was not the spontaneous visionary of the legend of Blake but in fact was a most laborious student of the literature of tradition and laid his foundations with immense strength and care.

In fact your prose works do serve another purpose in as much as they are also bridge of access to your poetry. A knowledge of your prose provides the supporting context to a reading of your poetry, so they have this double function, of leading to the larger world of tradition in general, and wherever the student wishes to take himself in that world, and also of leading to your poetry.

Well, I hope thats true because I often feel I should have written more poetry and less of this kind of scholarly labor that I've indulged in, but maybe I had to do this. It does rather seem to me that every poet of any quality is writing from deep studies of something or other. You can't just sit down and write poetry. A poet like Vernon Watkins had wide and deep foundations too. I think the trouble with the so-called poets nowadays is that they do not have this context out of which they are writing, so their work is very thin. It is only out of the day to day and immediate experience. I think

no one studied these matters more deeply than Yeats did, although I've probably read everything he read and some more as well by now. I regret it in a way. I really think that it would have been better to entrust myself more to the springs of life and perhaps less to these other studies. But I'm glad you think it provides a bridge of access for people, at least on that level.

You would agree then that for a poet of any imaginative depth at all, the modus operandi of poetic vision is a mastery of symbols.

Yes, most certainly. And when one has learnt the language of tradition, so to say which is a symbolic language, one can tell instantly whether a given poet is writing with knowledge of this language or without. It isn't a different language for every poet that you read; it is one language that runs right through the whole of European and to a certain extent world literature. One knows immediately when a poet uses the symbol of water, or whatever it may be, whether he is using it with these resonances of meaning or without. Milton, Coleridge, Shelley, Keats, for example. To a certain extent Edwin Muir, Vernon Watkins. One knows that this is the language which is being used. Or one might find a similar word in some non-traditional poet like Auden, and one can tell immediately that it is not being used in this sense. One then experiences this as a loss of resonance. The mastery of a traditional language is of great importance.

What would you say is the purpose of symbolic discourse?

Symbols speak to the soul. The psyche doesn't think in words; it is the temporal man, ego, that uses a verbal language. But a symbol which is finally grounded in nature reaches back to regions of experience that are far deeper than verbalization can ever reach. These symbols touch us at a much deeper level; they come from a deeper level and they speak to a deeper level. They strike these resonances. A symbol must be grounded in physical nature because that is where the form of the symbol comes from, but it also resonates in a vertical level, in the level of the soul, and possibly beyond that again at a metaphysical level. Therefore, while words are, as it were, a horizontal level of discourse, symbols are a vertical level, calling into play all the different levels of our humanity: life, spirit, the whole range of our human being. Of course, dead symbols are not doing so; they are then working simply at the level of consciousness like any other kind of verbalization. But when a symbol is living, it speaks to the whole being.And again, to return to Jung, whom I must defend, the soul receives its oracles in symbolic form, as for example in dreams, very seldom in verbal form.

Then the knowledge that symbols yield is an aid to spiritual regeneration?

Certainly. It's an awakening. They are the strongest possible agents of what Plato calls *anamnesis*, the unforgetting, the awakening of that in us which, according to Plato, we know but don't in fact know we know. Because the symbol speaks to that level, it has a far greater power of awakening the inner dimensions, our inner being, than word, than mere verbalizations which remain on the level of natural humanity living in a physical environment, the level of rational thought.

In a traditional society, symbolic knowledge gains its spiritual efficacy by being situated within a total metaphysical context.

Yes, if there ever were such a thing as this traditional society. I suspect it is an abstraction, that the situation is one that has never actually existed in any human society and is sort of the ideal point to which we refer ourselves. It does, of course, still exist for those who have understood and experienced in depth the symbols of any tradition, any religion. It is a possibility at all times, but a possibility for a whole society I should think never.

If we may take the example of Dante, for instance, he could rely, on the part of his reader, on the whole of scholastic cosmology, so that when he used a traditional symbol that symbol resonated in his reader. Now obviously the modern poet doesn't have this supportive context, so when he uses a traditional symbol what can he really hope to sound in his reader?

Insofar as he uses a traditional symbol that is part of a cultural inheritance, of course he can't sound anything, but insofar as the great symbols of tradition are themselves rooted in abiding reality itself, as light, water, the Great Mother, the Tree of Life, they come from human experience and they can speak again to human experience, if they are used with that intention. I think Yeats succeeded in using them in this way. But insofar as they belong to a cultural context, then, as we said earlier, I'm afraid the situation is very bad; they don't resonate.

Yes, it was this lack or this disappearance of a cultural context that concerned David Jones, wasn't it? I think it's this that makes him such a central figure in our time.

Yes, it concerned him very deeply. I think he did manage to use the Christian liturgy in a living way; he was probably the last great writer in this country who will be able to do so. I think it would be impossible for someone like myself, for example, to do so, although indeed David Gascoyne has used many of the central Christian symbols with a tremendous resonance, though not in a liturgical context. In a way he's removed them from the liturgical context in order to use them with that sense of nowness which the other David, David Jones, says is essential to any work of art. Yeats wrestled with this problem also, of what was available to him culturally. Of course he had Irish history and Irish mythology to a certain extent. He used certain symbols like Leda and the swan and gave them new power by his use of them. I think if these symbols are to be used it is for the poet to renew their power, as Rilke did, for example, with the symbol of angels or Holderlin with Greek mythology or Shelley. The power can be renewed if the poet is great enough, and then this restores in measure the past to the present. But merely to use them in a conventional manner expecting conventional response, that is no use at all; that's over. If the modern poet is doing so, it may well be that he is falling back not upon a living experience but upon book learning, in which case the symbol is not alive in the poem to begin with and therefore will not arouse any living response in the reader. Symbols are living things. I think Yeats understood very well that, as he puts it, "Things thought too long can be no longer thought." You can't go on repeating yourself, because art must always be new. If you are going to use a traditional symbol, it must come from the source of life itself; it mustn't only come from book learning or it will be simply repeating something that had validity in the past. And that, far from renewing a symbol, is the surest way to kill it. That is why so many of the symbols have died. But when a poet can take a symbol, relive it, and restore it to its original glory by reimmersing it in the source of life itself, as I think Yeats does with Leda and the swan, he brings it right back into our experience and present in a living way.

In The Lion's Mouth *you have suggested that it may be that our times are sweeping away the concept of the cult as spiritual support. What, other than some form of idolatry, can you see replacing it?*

What was expressed outwardly in the cult must be interiorized and experienced imaginatively. I'm afraid I can but give the answer that Blake gave, and that is that we must discover the God within, in the human imagination. Instead of looking for outside supports, look within, for God is in every created being, in ourselves, in one another, in the whole of nature. Once we've realized that, the whole, apparently external world becomes, as Blake says, "one continuous vision of imagination", communicating at every moment its meaning. Immediately. When the sun rises, when a flower opens — all of these are immediate communications of spiritual reality. That is an ideal situation but I think we are forced into this situation by the fact that there's nowhere else to go except within. And I think that is where we must go. This renews not only the inner world of dreams, which I think Jung very well understood, but it would have the effect also of renewing the outer world. When we experience the outer environment in a living way, it ceases to have this sort of inhuman deadness that it has for the materialist and becomes in itself a living experience. Blake believed that poetry, music, and painting were man's three ways of conversing with Paradise that the flood has not swept away, that this is the voice of Imagination, that true art which comes from the indwelling spirit of man is the voice of God. It is the voice of religion. In that sense, I think that Jung also played a great part in opening the inner worlds and pointing out to us the oracle that each of us has within the heart. The symbols presented to us in our own dreams and in our own living experience are living communications of the Divine. I know this is very dangerous. If one imagines, for example, taking the teachings of Christianity out of our world, the prospect is very grim indeed. But Jesus himself taught that the kingdom of heaven is within, and I can only see, as Blake did, that this is the religion of Jesus. The kingdom of heaven is within and must be discovered by us there, not projected as formerly into sacred forms and sacred formulae, which indeed did serve to awaken the inner response but no longer do so and are therefore useless. It is only insofar as the outer forms awaken the inner realization that they have any use; they have no other intrinsic validity. I can't see where else we can go, but I wouldn't want to be dogmatic on such an immense issue.

Would you agree that the erosion of spiritual boundaries that we see today can lead to the danger of arriving at a neo-theism, devoid of the integral support of a specific tradition?

I think that this is a great difficulty, but one must remember that symbols, wonderful as they are, are merely pointers that point towards realities. The things which are symbolized are enduring elements in human experience and in the cosmos itself and will not go away just because a certain symbolic language no longer serves to describe them. The realities abide. In the situation in which we are, there seem to be only two possibilities. One is the renewal of symbols by reimmersing ourselves in the source, a rediscovery of symbols from within. Or, we must remember that the God within is a living God, that every moment of our experience is just as close to the source as time past or time future. These things are realities; they are immediate. You may change the name, but you cannot remove the reality. You may abolish the cult of the Blessed Virgin Mary, but you will not by that undermine the reality of the Great Mother Goddess, the Feminine Principle, of whom the Blessed Virgin has stood for two thousand years as a valid symbol. She will be re-experienced; people will have dreams of her. I know people who have never been to church but who have had dreams of even Jesus Christ, because the figure of Jesus Christ, again, is the central divine humanity, under whatever name, to which we are all as human beings oriented. We can entrust ourselves to the real in the confidence that we cannot as human beings be totally removed from the source from which our life springs. Of course, disbelief is another thing; I think it is a very terrible situation in which the efficacy of the cult as a support for religious experience is removed from us. I quite agree with you that it is a very frightening prospect, but because the reality which is mediated by the cult remains, I think we must not despair. I can only give Blake's answer, and indeed Yeats's, that rather than through the cult we can experience these realities through poetry and the arts. After all, the cult is only a work of art, really, expressing certain imaginative experiences of a collective kind. It is a great mistake to think of the cult as being other than a great collective work of art. For example, the Cathedral of Chartres practically embodies the whole mystery of Christianity. You can take it as a religious symbol; you can take it as a work of art. There is no difference at that level.

And art should itself be rooted in the spiritual and eternal world. When Blake seeks to say that art is a religion, he did not mean at all that profane art can take the place of religion. He was trying to say that any supreme work of art is rooted in imaginative truth and revelation and is in that sense fulfilling the role which cult and liturgy fulfill in ages which can make use of these. And Yeats of course, who was not as good a Christian as he might have been but was a deeply religious man, held the same. I know this answer isn't satisfactory, but I think we have no alternative because the cult is going anyway. We know this. You and I have both, I'm sure, tried our best to make use of the cult and found it strangely irrelevant to our own deepest experience. And because we have no alternative, I think we are driven into seeking the God within; we have nowhere else to go.

On the basis of what you have said, can I now put to you a question which I feel is perhaps the most crucial of any that I've asked you this afternoon. If it is of the nature of symbols themselves that they have very specific psychological and religious connotations, and if one does away with the connotations when one does away with the cult, how can we use symbols at all without abandoning something of their real nature?

I'm afraid we're forced, however much we may try to escape, to the conclusion that we are living in the terminal phase of certainly a civilization, and perhaps a whole world of civilization. I remember Marco Pallis saying to me when I made a bitter complaint about Christendom, Christianity as a cult, that I need not imagine that other religious traditions were in any better shape, that the same was in fact happening in India and in the Far East and in other places. And he said, I remember, that you can't expect anything else at the end of the Kali Yuga. And in this terminal situation, I think it is useless to try to keep alive the corpse of civilization as we have known it. We have perhaps to undergo this spiritual death and rebirth. But one remembers the words of Jesus: "Heaven and earth shall pass away: but my word shall not pass away". The word of the logos, given to man, will endure as long as we ourselves endure. I see no alternative. Culturally, of course, I have to agree with you that there is very little hope. I wouldn't say no hope, because God has knowledge at his disposal that we ourselves lack. But insofar as I can see, speaking for myself, I see this as being the terminal phase of European Christendom—not of the teachings of Jesus Christ, but of the great culture, the cult, the whole story of man in the West for these two thousand years. I think it has reached its end. I see nowhere else that we can go except, as I say, within. You may have noticed that in my poems I rely more and more on nature, because I do truly believe in the words of the Jewish prayer, with which every Jew greets the day: "Praise be to thee, King of the universe, who new creates thy world every morning". So that is where I myself turn; it is to the immediate living experience of the living God, the God within humanity, whom Blake called "Jesus the Imagination", by which he meant the logos within man. This, I think, was what Blake found to be the great difference between the Jewish tradition, whose conception is of a living God with whom man walks, communicating at every moment, to which man is open and attentive, and the Greek tradition, which rather abstracts certain truths and sees it all as a great structure. When it comes to the final issue, all we have with certainty is the knowledge that our very existence rests upon the immediate creation of every moment that we live by this God within. And that comes down to the bare bones of things. But I think at that point, which may be the death of culture and civilization, there may be a rebirth in another dimension of which we as yet can see very little. All the poet can do is stand on the ground that remains.

The poet and artist do seem strangely to keep the intuitive channels open at a time when increasingly often the sacred seems closed to both theology and philosophy alike.

There have always been the prophets as well as the priests, which I think perhaps Guénon and his school somewhat have forgotten. The prophetic spirit which "blows where it listeth" is what Blake proclaimed, and he said that poet is only a modern word for prophet. And the prophets are those who speak for God. In other words, they speak not from the personal ego but from the imagination which is the God within all humanity. This is still so. It seems to be what we are left with, taking the function of the poet in the deepest sense, spiritually understood to be the prophetic utterance. Yeats, you remember, says that genius is a crisis that unites the sleeping and the waking mind, that gives entrance to the other mind beyond the mind of the ego. In so far as the poet or the painter or the musician can keep open this channel through which the spirit speaks, things which we have not yet imagined, which we cannot know, the spirit will speak to our age. There is always a message for every age. In that sense I am not despairing, as indeed it is not in the nature of the poet to despair of inspiration, because the reception of this spirit that blows where it listeth is precisely the task of any poet.

Brian Keeble writes, and runs the Golgonooza Press (3, Cambridge Drive, Ipswich, Suffolk, England IP2 9EP) which publishes 'works of poetry and prose which by their spirit and understanding foster a rapport between the spiritual criteria of the sacred traditions and the concerns of the practising contemporary artist.'

Kathleen Raine: A Selective Bibliography

Dr. Raine has published continuously since 1929. Since then poetry, essays, translations, reviews, introductions have flowed from her pen; by and for which she has lived; always trying, as she says, never to accept a task out of necessity that she could not, in some way, perform out of love. The following is a selective bibliography—a biography in writings, a guide to further study—drawn from the fuller but still preliminary checklist compiled by Alan Clodd of the Enitharmon Press and published in the *Ampleforth Journal* for Summer 1978 (Vol. LXXXIII Part II).

1929—First poems published: 'Chloris whenas I woo' and 'Hymn for the B.V.M' in *Experiment*, Nos 2 and 3.

1931—Poems included in: *'An Anthology of Cambridge Women's Verse'*, compiled by Margaret Thomas (Hogarth Press).

1935—Poems included in: *Poems of Tomorrow*, An Anthology of Contemporary Verse Chosen from *The Listener*, by Janet Adam Smith (Chatto and Windus).

1937—*May the Twelfth Mass-Observation Day-Surveys 1937*, edited by Humphrey Jennings, Charles Madge and...Kathleen Raine (Faber and Faber); poems included in: *The Year's Poetry* (John Lane).

1943—*Stone and Flower: poems 1935-43*, with 3 drawings by Barbara Hepworth (P.L. Nicholson and Watson).

1944—'Literature in the Modern World' in *This Changing World*, edited by J. R. M. Brumwell (George Routledge).

1945—*Talk of the Devil* by Denis de Rougement translated by Kathleen Raine (Eyre and Spottiswoode).

1946—*Living in Time* (Editions Poetry London).

1947—*Aspects de la Littérature Anglaise 1918-45*, edited by Kathleen Raine and Max-Pol Fouchet (Paris: Editions de la Revue Fontaine).

1948—*Cousine Bette* by Honoré de Balzac, translated by Kathleen Raine (Hamish Hamilton Novel Library); *Existentialism* by Paul Foulquie, translated by Kathleen Raine (Dennis Dobson).

1949—*The Pythoness and other poems* (Hamish Hamilton). (U. S. Edition, Random House 1952).

1950—*The Letters of Samuel Tayler Coleridge*, selected and with an introduction by Kathleen Raine (Grey Walls Press); 'Michael Roberts and the Hero Myth' in *Penguin New Writing* no 39.

1951—*Poemas*. Selección, versión y prólogo de M. Manent. Colección Adonais no LXXV (Madrid: Editions Rialp); *Lost Illusions* by Honoré de Balzac, translated by Kathleen Raine (Lehman); *William Blake*: Writers and their Work no 12 (British Council and the National Book League); 'Introduction' in *Poems by Humphrey Jennings* (New York: Weekend Press).

1952—*Selected Poems* (New York: Weekend Press); *The Year One and Other Poems* (Hamish Hamilton). (U.S. Edition, Farrar, Strauss and Young 1953)

1953—*Coleridge*: Writers and their Work no 43 (British Council and the National Book League).

1954—'The Symbol and the Rose' in *Highlights of Modern Literature* edited by Francis Brown (New York:New American Library); 'Who Made the Tyger?' in *Encounter*, II.6.

1956—*The Collected Poems of Kathleen Raine* (Hamish Hamilton). (U. S. Edition, Random House). (French Translation: *Isis Errante*, by Francois Xavier Jaujard. Paris: Granit 1978).

1957—*Samuel Taylor Coleridge, Poems and Prose*, selected with an introduction by Kathleen Raine (Harmonsworth: Penguin Books); 'The Little Girl Lost and Found and the Lapsed Soul' in *The Divine Vision: Studies in the Poetry and Art of William Blake* edited by Vivian de Sola Pinto (Gollancz).

1958—'Poetry in Relation to Traditional Wisdom' (Guild of Pastoral Psychology Lecture no 97); 'Some Sources of Tiriel' in *The Huntington Library Quarterly* vol 21.

1960—'Blake and England' (Cambridge: W. Heffer). The Girton College Founders' Memorial Lecture.

1961—'The Responsibility of the Poet' (Centre for Spiritual and Psychological Studies); 'Edwin Muir: an Appreciation' in *The Texas Quarterly* vol IV no 3.

1963—'The Poetic Symbol' (Centre for Spiritual and Psychological Studies); 'Blake's Debt to Antiquity' in *The Sewanee Review* vol LXXI no 3.

1964—*The Golden Cantata*: Poems by Kathleen Raine: Music by Arthur Bliss (Novello and Co); 'Introduction' in *Letters on Poetry from W. B. Yeats to Dorothy Wellesley* (Oford University Press); 'The Poetic Symbol and Tradition' in *Tomorrow* vol 12, no 3; 'Vernon Watkins: Poet of Tradition' in *The Texas Quarterly* vol VII, no 2; 'Symbolism in 'Kubla Khan' ' in *The Sewanee Review* vol LXXII, no 4.

1965—*The Hollow Hill and other poems 1960-1964* (Hamish Hamilton); 'The Poetic Symbol' in *the Southern Review* vol I (new series), no 2.

1966—'The Use of the Beautiful' in *The Southern Review* vol II (new series), no 2.

1967—*Defending Ancient Springs* (Oxford University Press); 'David Gascoyne and the Prophetic Role' in *The Sewanee Review* vol LXXV, no 2; 'A Defense of Shelley's Poetry' in *The Southern Review* vol III (new series), no 4; 'Yeats and Platonism' in *The Texas Quarterly* vol X, no 4.

1968—*Selected Poems* (Pergamon Press); *Blake and Tradition*: The A. W. Mellon Lectures in the Fine Arts, 1962. Bollinger Series XXXV.11 (Princeton University Press) 2 vols; (English Edition, Routledge 1969); *Life's a Dream*, a play in three acts by Calderon, translated by Kathleen Raine and R. M. Nadal (Hamish Hamilton); 'Blake and Education' (Centre for Spiritual and Educational Studies); 'Thomas Taylor, Plato and the English Romantic Movement' in *The Sewanee Review* vol LXXVI, no 2, and *The British Journal of Aesthetics* vol 8, no 2; 'Intuition's Lightning: the Poetry of Vernon Watkins' in *The Poetry Review* vol XIX, no 1.

1969—'Thomas Taylor in England' in *Selected Writings of Thomas Taylor, the Platonist* edited and introduced by Kathleen Raine and George Mills Harper (Princeton University Press/Bollingen Series); 'Herbert Read as a Literary Critic' in *The Malahat Review no 9 and* The Sewanee Review vol LXXVII no 3; 'Yeats, the Tarot and the Golden Dawn' in *The Sewanee Review* vol LXXVII no 1.

1970—'Selected Poems' in *Penguin Modern Poets no 17* (Harmondsworth: Penguin); *William Blake* (Thames and Hudson World of Art Library); (French Edition, translated by Nicole Tisserand and Michel Oriano, Paris: Editions de Chêne, 1975); 'Poetic Symbols as a Vehicle of Tradition: The Crisis of the Present in English Poetry' in *Polaritat des Lebens*—Eranos Jahrbuch XXXVII/1968 (Zurich: Rhein-Verlag); 'Herbert Read as a Literary Critic' in *Herbert Read: A Memorial Symposium* edited by Robin Skelton (Methuen and Co).

1971—*The Lost Country* (The Dolmen Press and Hamish Hamilton); 'Blake's Last Judgment' *The Ampleforth Journal* LXXVI.2; 'From the Faces of Day and Night' in *The Malahat Review*, no 18.

1972—*Yeats, the Tarot and the Golden Dawn* (Dublin: The Dolmen Press); *Faces of Day and Night* (Enitharmon Press(; 'Blake and the Present Generation' in *The Ampleforth Journal* LXXVII.2; 'Hopkins—Nature and Human Nature' (The Hopkins Society). (The Third Annual Hopkins Lecture: Printed by Stanbrook Abbey Press).

1973—*Farewell, Happy Fields: Memories of Childhood* (Hamish Hamilton); (U. S. Edition, George Braziller, 1977); (French Edition, *Adieu Prairies Heureuses*, Préface de Diane de Margerie, Paris: Stock, 1978); *On a Deserted Shore* (Dublin: The Dolmen Press and Hamish Hamilton); (French Edition, *Sur un Rivage Désert*, translated by Marie-Beatrice Mesnet and Jean Mainbrino S.J., Paris: Granit, 1978); 'Foreword' to *Fairy and Folk Tales of Ireland*, edited by w. b. yeats (Gerrards Cross: Colin Smythe); 'Introduction' to *Selected Poems of Shelley* (Harmondsworth: Penguin).

1974—'Wordsworth and Blake: two views on nature' in *The Ampleforth Journal LXXIX.1*; 'David Jones: Solitary Perfectionist' (Ipswich: The Golgonooza Press); (Enlarged edition, 1975); *Death-in-Life and Life-in-Death: 'Cuchulain Comforted' and 'News for the Delphic Oracle'* (Dublin: Dolmen Press).

1975—*The Land Unknown: Further Chapters of Autobiography* (Hamish Hamilton); (U. S. Edition, with different introduction, George Braziller); 'Hades Wrapped in Cloud' in *Yeats and the Occult*, edited by George Mills Harper (MacMillan, Canada); 'AE' in *Light*, vol 95, nos 1 and 2.

1976—'The Inner Journey of the Poet' (Ipswich: The Golgonooza Press); 'Berkeley, Blake and the New Age' (Ipswich: The Golgonooza Press; and *Thought*, New York); 'The Inner Journey of the Poet II' in *Light* vol 96, no 1; '12 Poems' in *The Malahat Review*, no 38; 'Blake's Christ-Consciousness' in *Studies in Comparative Religion*, Autumn.

1977—*The Oval Portrait and other poems* (Enitharmon Press and Hamish Hamilton); *The Lion's Mouth: Concluding Chapters of Autobiography* (Hamish Hamilton); (U. S. Edition, George Braziller, 1978); 'Foreword' to *The Fairy Faith in Celtic Countries* by W. Y. Evans Wentz (Gerrards Cross: Colin Smythe).

1978—*Blake and Antiquity* (Princeton/Bollingen); 'David Jones: The Actually Loved and Known' (Ipswich: The Golgonooza Press).

1979—*From Blake to a Vision* (Dublin: The Dolmen Press); *The Oracle in the Heart* (Dublin: The Dolmen Press).

CREDITS AND ACKNOWLEDGEMENTS

We would like to thank the following for their generosity in freely making available copyright material for this issue of the Lindisfarne Newsletter:

Brian Keeble, for his Interview with Kathleen Raine;

Alan Clodd, for the use of his Bibliography of Kathleen Raine;

the British Academy for 'Waste Land, Holy Land';

Hamish Hamilton for 'Lenten Flowers', 'Isis Wanderer', 'The Herm', 'Pythoness' from *The Collected Poems of Kathleen Raine*, and for 'Eudaimon', 'Rose', 'Statues', 'Triad', from *The Hollow Hill*;

The Dolmen Press and Hamish Hamilton for 'Heirloom', 'I felt, under my old breasts, this April day', 'Judas-Tree' from *The Lost Country*, and the poems numbered 13, 14, 82, 100 from *On A Deserted Shore;*

The Enitharmon Press and Hamish Hamilton for 'Blue butterflies' eyed wings', 'Sorrow, Sorrow', 'Harvest of Learning I have reaped', 'Bright Cloud' from *The Oval Portrait and other poems;*

and, of course, Kathleen Raine, for everything.

Pictures and credits:

front cover—ivory *pyxis* in Bobbio, said to have been the gift of St. Gregory to Columban, in *Orpheus and Greek Religion,* W. K. C. Guthrie, Norton 1966;

title-page—vase-painting of Orpheus, in *Prologomena to the Study of Greek Religion,* J. E. Harrison, Meridian Books 1955;

contents page—drawing of shaman, in *Studies in Siberian Shamanism,* edited by H. N. Michael, University of Toronto Press 1963;

page 11—the staff of Hermes from a drawing by Hans Holbein the Younger, in *Alchemy,* T. Burckhardt, Penguin 1971;

page 15—tarot card "The World", in *The Mystical Tower of the Tarot,* J. D. Blakeley, Watkins 1974;

page 28—pictish cross from Glamis, in *The Early Christian and Pictish Monuments of Scotland,* S. Cruden, H.M.S.O. 1964;

page 33—Dionysos, in *Prologomena to the Study of Greek Religion,* J. E. Harrison, Meridian Books, 1955;

page 34—the vision of the prophet Ezekiel from a twelfth century English manuscript illumination, in *The Hero,* D. Norman, World Publishing Company 1969;

page 51—emblem of Isis, from Bryant's *Mythology,* in *Blake and Tradition,* K. Raine, Princeton 1968;

pages 52 to 74—vase-painting of Apollo, in *Themis,* J. E. Harrison, University Books, 1962;

inside back cover—boss from interior arcade, St. Mary's Chapel, Glastonbury Abbey, in *Abbeys,* M. R. James, Great Western Railway, Paddington Station 1926.

Special thanks to N. Haydn Stubbing for his drawing on page 79.

NEWS OF THE ASSOCIATION

Lindisfarne has been talking about decentralization ever since E. F. Schumacher first visited us in 1974; now, finally, we will have a chance to live it. Rather than having one single center in the world center of New York City, Lindisfarne is going to be spinning off its activities into several different areas of the country.

The Lindisfarne Press has been established on a farm in the Berkshires of Western Massachusetts; there Christopher and Diane Bamford, René Guzmán-Ortiz, and Will Marsh will administer the Corresponding Membership Program, distribute the Lindisfarne Tapes, continue to publish the Lindisfarne Letter, and begin to publish a new series of books. Individuals interested in becoming Corresponding Members, or in ordering publications, should write to the Lindisfarne Press, R.D.2, West Stockbridge, Massachusetts 01266.

The Lindisfarne Conferences, as well as the meetings of the Lindisfarne Fellows, will take place at the Zen Center Green Gulch Farm in Marin County, California. To provide the necessary guest facilities for these meetings, a Lindisfarne Fellows House is being built on the monastery's farm. Our first conference at Green Gulch, a seminar on sacred architecture, was held from June 18 to 22 of this year.

A new Lindisfarne Institute is being established in the Sangre de Cristo Mountains of southern Colorado. In its first year this group will be concerned with the "Meta-industrial Village Project," which is a village-level approach to appropriate technology, and research and construction in a special program of Sacred Architecture.

Eventually, a monastic retreat and study center will be built on the foothills within sight of the sacred mountain revered by the Indians of the Southwest, Mt. Blanca. The members of the Association who will be involved with this project will be Amory Lovins, Maurice Strong and William Irwin Thompson, as residents; and Mary Catherine Bateson, Kieth Critchlow, and John and Nancy Todd as consultants. More information about the program in Sacred Architecture and the Meta-industrial Village project of the Lindisfarne Institute in Colorado will be published in the next issue of the Lindisfarne Letter.

The general offices of the Lindisfarne Association will be at the Cathedral Church of Saint John the Divine, 1047 Amsterdam Avenue, New York, N.Y. 10025.

* * *

A new title in the Lindisfarne Series of books published by Harper and Row will appear in October. The work is *Tomorrow Is Our Permanent Address* by John and Nancy Todd, Lindisfarne Fellows and Co-Directors of The New Alchemy Institute in Woods Hole, Massachusetts. The book is concerned with the theory and design of arks and bioshelters, or semi-closed ecological systems; and the more general cultural implications these new forms of symbiotic architecture have for a world struggling to find an alternative to nuclear arms and energy.

*

Mind and Nature: a Necessary Unity by Gregory Bateson has been published by E. P. Dutton. This book was written at Lindisfarne when Gregory Bateson was our Fellow-in-Residence in 1977. It is a work of major significance and all of us who were privileged to have heard the early versions of the book in Gregory's lectures at Lindisfarne from 1975 to 1977 feel a keen sense of involvement in this work.

*   *

A Note to Our Members

As mentioned on the preceding page, under our new set-up the Corresponding Membership program will be administered by the Lindisfarne Press in West Stockbridge, Massachusetts. Will Marsh has been designated as the person responsible for the care and development of the program, so any questions or comments about membership should be directed to him. Corresponding Memberships are the chief source of support for the Lindisfarne Letter, although we may occasionally receive a most-welcome large contribution to underwrite a specific issue. The best way that you can help us is by telling others about our work. Word-of-mouth is our best source of new contacts and support. Your help does make a difference, and we are most thankful for it.

*   *   *

BLUE BUTTERFLIES' EYED WINGS

Blue butterflies' eyed wings,
Eyed buzzard high in blue sky,
Mountain isles blue veiled
In fleeting shade of fleeting cloud,
Of these I am the I.

Kathleen Raine